LET'S JUST Laugh AT THAT!

By Steve Backlund

With

Phil Drysdale

Chuck Maher

Kim McGan

Jared Neusch

This book is dedicated to my mother, Lynn Backlund. She has influenced me more than any person to love God and to share Him with others. Thanks, Mom, for the difference you have made. You are loved!

Acknowledgements

Special assistance: Wendy Backlund, Madeline Guzo, Leslie Taylor

Front and Back Cover Design: Linda Lee

ISBN: 978-0-578-08074-1

Endorsements for <u>Let's Just Laugh at That</u>!

<u>Let's Just Laugh at That!</u> is the appropriate title for the latest book from Steve Backlund. In it, he trains believers to take on the mind of Christ and see the devil's lies from God's perspective. I love Steve's continual efforts to bring encouragement and strength to the body of Christ. This book is sure to be a source of great refreshing. **Bill Johnson, Senior Pastor of Bethel Church in Redding, California, Author of <u>When Heaven Invades Earth</u>**

In <u>Let's Just Laugh At That!</u> you will find great bite-sized truths that will nourish you into the fullness of your destiny. **Kevin Dedmon, author of <u>The Ultimate Treasure Hunt</u>**

Steve's ministry has changed my personal and ministry life. What he has done with this book is translate his message to paper and create a very practical approach to a joy filled and victorious Christian life. Many people teach and write, but a few actually change the way we live! Steve has done it again!! This book will change your personal, ministry and organizational life by the simple exposing of lies and releasing the Kingdom emotion of joy over them. **Paul Manwaring, Overseer of Global Legacy, Bethel Church, Redding**

As an inner healing and deliverance minister, I am constantly helping others expose and exchange the lies they are believing for the truth of God's word. <u>Let's Just Laugh at That!</u> is a powerful, fun book that will challenge you to daily renew your mind, and position you to walk laughingly through any struggle you face. **Dawna De Silva, Sozo Ministry Founder and Transformation Center Ministries' Coordinator at Bethel Church, Redding, California.**

Joy warfare is the tactical strategy of the hour. Bible translator, J. B Phillips said, "distrust your religion if it is grumpy..." In <u>Let's Just Laugh at That!</u> Steve Backlund and his unquenchable interns inject us with the joy anti-venom to stop the deadly poison of grumpy religion. While laughing my way through these pages, I felt like I was reading Gods offensive and defensive playbook for triumphant living. These forty-five lie detectors perform a polygraph test on your thinking to reveal whether you are enjoying your privilege of a renewed mind. Read through this book often and allow it to perform a vital virus scan on your belief systems and update your operating system to the freshest version of the overcoming life. **Dan (Dano) McCollam – The Mission, Vacaville, California. Director of Sounds of the Nations and faculty for Bethel's School of Worship and School of the Prophets, Redding, California.**

I served underneath Steve Backlund in one of the greatest learning seasons of my life as a leader. I am so thankful for this season because of what Steve taught and lived. This book contains some of the key things that I learned – which includes to laugh a lot, and I mean a lot!!! This is a must read. **Eric Johnson, Senior Overseer at Bethel School of Supernatural Ministry, Redding**

Table of Contents

About the Authors

Steve Backlund

Steve and Wendy Backlund from Bethel Church in Redding, California, have a unique ministry that ignites passion, joy, victorious mindsets and healthy relationships. They minister a message of hope, vision and faith; as well as imparting keys for effective, joy-filled leadership. They were senior leaders of renewal churches from 1991 to 2008 (Round Mountain, Nevada, and Weaverville, California). The Backlunds travel regularly ministering to churches and leadership teams. They have three grown children and four grandchildren. Steve has authored six other books. Learn more about his books and other resources at www.ignitedhope.com and on his Facebook page (Ignited Hope Ministries).

Steve's 2010-11 Interns Helped Write This Book

Phil Drysdale

Phil is originally from Scotland and served as Steve's personal assistant while interning at Bethel School of Supernatural Ministry. His heart is to see people come into a revelation of the goodness of God and their perfection in Christ through hearing an undiluted gospel of grace. He loves life and is presently living in Redding, California.

Chuck Maher

Chuck is from Newbrunswick, Canada and is a graduate of Bethel School of Supernatural Ministry in Redding, California. He served as Steve Backlund's Travel Intern from September, 2010-May, 2011. Chuck's desire is to see the church walk in its true identity, bringing cultural transformation throughout the earth.

Kim McGan

Kim assisted Steve in the Church Leadership and Planting track in the Bethel School of Supernatural Ministry. She is originally from Kentucky. She has a great passion to awaken believers into a lifestyle of intimacy and habitual victory and joy. She desires to see city-wide transformation take place in every city and in every nation. Her dream is to directly, or indirectly, impact the lives of a billion people.

Jared Neusch

Jared assists Steve with the Leadership Development Program in Global Legacy. In addition to supporting Steve, he is also on staff in Global Legacy at Bethel Church. He is originally from Texas and his heart has always been for the church to succeed. He most comes alive when he teaches, travels, and writes.

Truths to Help Understand This Book

Truth brings hope – "Now may the God of hope fill you with all joy and peace in believing" (Romans 15:13). Hope fills us at the moment we believe truth. Hope is the confident expectation that good is coming. Our hope level is the indicator of whether we believe truth or lies. Our hopelessness about a problem is a bigger problem than the problem. There are no hopeless circumstances, only hopeless people. Once someone gets true hope, the circumstance cannot stay the same.

The battle is between truth and lies – "The truth shall make you free" (John 8:32). The kingdom of God is not primarily moved forward by good conduct, but by good beliefs. The New Covenant believer is to be more belief-focused than conduct–focused. We can have great doctrine concerning the foundations of the faith, but still be spiritually weak because we believe lies.

Renewing our minds now transforms future experience – We transform our tomorrow by renewing our minds today (Romans 12:2). We don't need a new set of circumstances as much as we need a new set of beliefs. The flow of power and blessing is blocked when we believe lies. Personal and situational transformation results from intentionally renewing our minds with truth. The question of the hour is not "Lord, tell me what to do," but it is "Lord, tell me what to believe." Right believing will cause right doing and a transformed experience in the promises of God.

"God laughs in heaven" (Psalm 2:4) – What is God laughing at in this Psalm? He is chuckling at what His enemies are saying and planning. We can become more like God by laughing with Him at the ridiculousness of Satan's lies. The phrase "Let's just laugh at that" has the unusual ability to take the power out of demonic deceptions (and then prepare the soil of our hearts for truth).

We have to let go of something in order to laugh – Just as disagreeing family members have to let go of something to laugh together, Christians often have to let go of manipulation, bitterness and/or unbelief to laugh.

Who told you that? – God asked Adam this in Genesis 3:11. It is an important question for us too after we declare something that is contrary to God's perspective about circumstances or our own identity.

Walk in love and wisdom as you live a joy-filled life – We are to "Rejoice with those who rejoice, and weep with those who weep" (Romans 12:15). We need to be sensitive to where people are at, and to what is going on in their lives, as we seek to bring joy to others.

How to Get the Most Out of This Book

Understand the five components of each page:

The primary lie to laugh at – This is a "kingpin" lie that limits God's ability to work in the lives of many. We urge you to read the lie out loud and then laugh audibly. Something powerful occurs when the falsehood is brought into the light.

The laughable assumptions – We have provided a list of "laughable assumptions" to assist in exposing how preposterous the primary lie is. This will help overcome any lingering deception that the primary lie actually may be true.

The truth – "The truth shall make you free" (John 8:32). We cannot simply get rid of a lie, but it must be replaced with truth. In this section, biblical examples and promises are provided to refute the primary lie and the assumptions behind it.

Strategies for overcoming this lie – Each teaching provides at least three helpful steps to accelerate transformation in the area of life that the lie addresses.

Declarations to renew your mind – "Faith comes by hearing" (Romans 10:17). A main way to renew our minds is to declare the truth into our own hearing. Remember, Jesus did not think His way out of the wilderness. Rather, He spoke truth to counteract challenges concerning His identity and the nature of His Father (Matthew 4:1-11). Declarations will help us do the same.

Immerse yourself in this book in these four ways:

1. Read it straight through to get saturated with its truth.
2. Read it as a personal daily devotional.
3. Read one page a day with family members. Laugh together, declare together and discuss the truths and strategies presented.
4. Participate in a group study using this book.

Read Steve's book Possessing Joy for the biblical and medicinal basis for pursuing a life of joy and laughter.

Indeed, joy and laughter are not optional components of the Christian life that is only for certain personalities, but are a vital factor for the strength and longevity we are called to walk in. Possessing Joy will help take the truths of Let's Just Laugh at That to whole new levels.

Let's Just Laugh at This Lie
It Is Not My Personality to Be Joyful or to Laugh Much

Laughable Assumptions Behind This Lie:
- ➤ Joy is an optional fruit of the Spirit and is only for certain personalities.
- ➤ The Bible was speaking only metaphorically when it said that a merry heart is good medicine.
- ➤ Just as some don't have the right personality to be a loving person, I don't have the personality to be a joyful person.
- ➤ God regrets giving man a sense of humor.
- ➤ We should not trust the perspective of any Christian who laughs a lot.
- ➤ It is okay to cry in church, but laughter should be avoided and shunned.
- ➤ I cannot be joyful until my circumstances change.

The Truth: We all can, and to need to, walk in abundant joy and laughter.
1) The joy of the Lord is truly our strength (Nehemiah 8:10). 2) Laughter improves our health (Proverbs 17:22). Many scientific studies confirm that a merry heart is indeed good like medicine. (See my book Possessing Joy for insight on this.) 3) As we become more like Jesus, we will experience more joy. "These things I have spoken to you, that My joy may remain in you, and *that* your joy may be full" (John 15:11). 4) "In [God's] presence is fullness of joy" (Psalm 16:11). We may not always be fully joyful in God's presence; but if we never are, we might not be in His presence as much as we think. I don't write this to bring guilt, but to help increase our expectation of joy manifesting as we pursue God.

Strategies for Overcoming This Lie:
1. **Know that God never commands us to do something that He does not give the grace to do** – If joy and laughter are valuable for the believer (which they are), then there is grace available to walk in each. It may take us a while, but we will learn if we don't give up.
2. **Receive by faith, not by feeling** – Many think that if they don't feel something happening in them, then nothing is happening to them. This thinking is backwards. God's pattern is that we believe and then experience, not experience and then believe (Mark 11:24).
3. **Value childlikeness and pursue the manifestation of joy in your life** – "Rejoice with those who rejoice, and weep with those who weep" (Romans 12:15). Yes, we don't laugh at all times, but it is still vital for us. Joy is not the whole pie, but it is an important piece for the Christian.

Declarations to Renew Your Mind: 1) God's joy is my strength. 2) My daily, hearty laughter is part of my plan for health, strength and longevity. 3) I encounter God by faith, not feelings.

Let's Just Laugh at This Lie
There Are No Solutions for This Situation

Laughable Assumptions Behind This Lie:

> ➤ This situation is so bad that even prayer is pointless.
> ➤ The devil has won a complete victory; therefore, resistance is futile.
> ➤ God cannot work this situation for good in the lives impacted by it.
> ➤ God does not have any wisdom for what should be done.
> ➤ Breakthrough is always difficult and will take a long time.
> ➤ God is angry and does not want to help those involved.

The Truth: God makes a way where there seems to be no way. 1) The Red Sea parted when it looked hopeless (Exodus 14). 2) God had a plan to defeat Goliath that no one was aware of (1 Samuel 17). 3) Bitter waters were surprisingly made sweet with the unlikely solution of throwing a tree into them (Exodus 15:22-27). 4) God defied logic by shutting a lion's mouth to protect Daniel (Daniel 6:22). 5) The three Hebrew children were supernaturally protected in the fire when it looked hopeless (Daniel 3:19-25). 6) Jesus multiplied food when provision was limited (Luke 9:10-17). 7) A famine ended in a day (2 Kings 7). 8) Money needed to pay taxes was found in the unusual location of a fish's mouth (Matthew 17:24-27).

Strategies for Overcoming This Lie:

1. **Believe there is always a way** – "God *is* faithful, who will not allow you to be tempted beyond what you are able, but with the temptation will also make the way of escape, that you may be able to bear *it*" (1 Corinthians 10:13). There is a way out of a mess and a way into victory. Believing that will draw to you the answers needed (James 1:5-8).

2. **Implement the power of Romans 8:28** – "And we know that all things work together for good to those who love God, to those who are the called according to *His* purpose" (Romans 8:28). God has a supernatural ability to work everything for good in the life of the believer.

3. **Feed your hope on testimonies of those who have overcome your situation and from those who have overcome great odds in life** – Encourage yourself by discovering that there are people who have come out of what you are facing (and even more difficult situations).

Declarations to Renew Your Mind: 1) God is working things for good in this situation. 2) God is revealing to me a powerful step to take concerning this. 3) A miracle will happen concerning this situation.

Let's Just Laugh at This Lie
Good Things Can't Last

Laughable Assumptions Behind This Lie:

➤ The Christian life is meant to be a constant struggle.

➤ Satan's attacks are more powerful than God's promises.

➤ People who experience breakthrough should brace themselves for the inevitable and unstoppable counterattack of the devil.

➤ We are not worthy of being continually blessed and protected.

➤ I am blessed now, but the rug will be pulled out from under me soon.

➤ I can only grow and learn through suffering and pain.

The Truth: God's goodness is to increasingly manifest in us so that the kingdom can manifest through us. 1) Psalm 91 reveals a supernatural protection for God's people, and we now live in a better covenant with better promises (Hebrews 8:6). 2) Satan's stealing and destroying was defeated on the cross (Colossians 2:15). 3) Jesus became a curse so that we would not have to experience the curse of constant difficulty (Galatians 3:13-14). 4) God has a progressively good purpose for our lives that moves us from glory to glory, strength to strength, and faith to faith (2 Corinthians 3:18; Psalm 84:7; Romans 1:17).

Strategies for Overcoming This Lie:

1. **Believe that you must be increasingly blessed to accomplish God's will** – The Great Commission of Matthew 28:18-20 cannot be done without an abundance of health, energy, finances, favor, wisdom, power, love and protection. Realize, too, that your breakthrough into blessing will cause others to increase and make a difference.

2. **Overcome spiritual warfare teachings that infer that difficulty is normal for the strong Christian** – The wise Christian thinks primarily about what God has done through Christ rather than what Satan is supposedly doing. Remember, whatever you focus on will increase. If you talk about being under spiritual attack, you will see more attacks. If you focus on divine protection, you will see more protection.

3. **Defeat the spirit of unworthiness that frequently sabotages blessings** – The "I don't deserve to be blessed" belief reduces many Christians back into lack and mediocrity. Let's put great spiritual effort into comprehending the wonder of our salvation. It will make a huge difference in our ability to sustain blessing and revival.

Declarations to Renew Your Mind: 1) God's blessings are increasing in my life. 2) In Christ, I am worthy to walk in all of God's blessings. 3) I have an abundance to accomplish every good work.

Let's Just Laugh at This Lie
It Is Too Late for My Children

Laughable Assumptions Behind This Lie:

> ➤ It is impossible for miracles to happen in the lives of my children.
> ➤ Past and current prayers are not effective concerning my children.
> ➤ My mistakes as a parent make it impossible for them to change.
> ➤ God's power and wisdom cannot overcome the mess they've created.
> ➤ God's promises for my family are untrue because of my shortcomings.
> ➤ Others may not be hopeless, but my children are.
> ➤ God is not putting any strong Christians in my children's lives.

The Truth: God is working powerfully in the lives of wayward children. 1) He brought Samson back to a place of commitment and impact—even after there was complete compromise in his life (Judges 16). 2) The Prodigal Son also seemed hopeless, but he came to his senses and returned to his father's house (Luke 15:11-32). 3) Mankind became wayward through Adam's rebellion, but God's pursuit of bringing all of us back into relationship with Him proves His heart to tenaciously pursue all, including our children.

Strategies for Overcoming This Lie:

1. **Realize that hopelessness concerning our children is a bigger problem than what is happening with our children** – Hopelessness fuels unbelief instead of faith, begging instead of declaring, and spirits of heaviness instead of eager anticipation to see God's promises fulfilled. The lack of hope must be confronted with truth and zeal.

2. **Know your covenant with God includes your children** – In response to the Philippian jailer's question of "What must I do to be saved?" Paul said, "Believe on the Lord Jesus Christ, and you will be saved, you and your household" (Acts 16:30-34). We can infer from this that our whole family will come under divine favor and influence because of our covenant with God.

3. **Keep growing in the Lord** – Instead of putting your prime spiritual energy into begging God to touch your children, focus primarily on demonstrating the life, love and power of God in such a way that your children will want what you have. Remember that God's plan for bringing your children back to Him is through a revelation of His goodness (Romans 2:4).

Declarations to Renew Your Mind: 1) God is revealing His goodness to my children. 2) God is working powerfully in the lives of my children. 3) My children's salvation is part of my covenant with God.

Let's Just Laugh at This Lie

I Am Not Physically Attractive Enough to Be Significant

Laughable Assumptions Behind This Lie:

➢ My physical flaws define who I am, and everyone looks better than me.

➢ Only very beautiful and handsome people can truly be happy.

➢ God only uses people who are physically attractive.

➢ Those who have good looks have lesser problems in life.

➢ Being "sexy" is absolutely necessary for happiness and influence.

➢ Nobody, but me, struggles with negative feelings about their looks.

➢ If I am overweight at all, then I should feel miserable about myself.

The Truth: There are qualities much more important than physical attractiveness. 1) Loving God – "Man looks at the outward appearance, but the LORD looks at the heart" (1 Samuel 16:7). 2) Having faith – "But without faith *it is* impossible to please *Him*" (Hebrews 11:6). 3) Loving others – "But [if I] have not love, it profits me nothing" (1 Corinthians 13:3). 4) Having integrity and making godly decisions – "Blessed [happy] *are* those who hear the word of God and keep it" (Luke 11:28).

Strategies for Overcoming This Lie:

1. **Focus on inner beauty, and it will help make you attractive to others** – Moses' face shone because he was in the presence of God (Exodus 34:29-35). The psalmist said, "They looked to Him and were radiant" (Psalm 34:5). Jesus, too, glowed and became increasingly attractive as He was transfigured by the presence of God (Mark 9:1-8).

2. **Prioritize accepting and loving yourself** – We cannot afford to have any thought about ourselves that God does not have about us. We must break off any lingering self-hatred in us so that we can truly love others in the same way that we love ourselves (Mark 12:31).

3. **Realize that "supermodel" or "hunk" looks can actually create temptations that you don't want to face** – Just as an abundance of money in the hands of someone without strong core values can cause increased temptation, so can beauty apart from character and strong morals. We need to overcome the delusion that those who are beautiful by the world's standards are automatically happier.

Declarations to Renew Your Mind: 1) My beauty on the inside makes me attractive to the right people on the outside. 2) My face shines because of the presence of God in my life. 3) I have a healthy self-image that creates favor on my life. 4) I am not intimidated by those who are apparently more beautiful than me, but I bless them and am a strength in their lives.

Let's Just Laugh at This Lie

Fear of Punishment Is How God Primarily Motivates Us

Laughable Assumptions Behind This Lie:

➢ What Christ did on the cross may have saved me from my sins, but I still deserve to be punished for them.

➢ Parents and God need to create a climate of fear or else sin will increase.

➢ I only learn and mature through fear, pain and suffering.

➢ A revelation of God's goodness does not lead people to repentance.

➢ God's love does not change people, but the fear of punishment will.

➢ People respond best to threats of punishment.

The Truth: A revelation of God's love is the New Covenant's motivation of people. 1) The Prodigal's father motivated him by showing him love (Luke 15:11-32). 2) God inspired Abraham with extravagant promises, not ramifications for not following Him (Genesis 12:1-3). 3) The adulterous woman was empowered to "sin no more" by forgiveness (John 8:1-11). 4) Jesus told Simon the Pharisee that those who understand how much they are loved and forgiven by God will have a correlating inner compulsion to extravagantly love God (Luke 7:39-50).

Strategies for Overcoming This Lie:

1. **Remind yourself of God's love for you** – God really loves you! He even likes you! He calls you friend (John 15:15) and son (Galatians 3:26). A true friend or father does not motivate others by threats of punishment. In fact, "there is no fear in [perfect] love" as it has been cast out (1 John 4:18).

2. **Believe God desires to motivate us by His goodness** – It is the revelation of God's goodness that causes repentance leading to transformation. "The goodness of God leads you to repentance" (Romans 2:4). Yes, we can learn wisdom through the pain of bad choices, but that is not God's highest way for us to grow and learn.

3. **Know that Jesus was punished for you so you wouldn't have to be** – Jesus took the punishment we deserve (Isaiah 53:4-7). It would be absolutely unjust for a just God to pour out punishment on a people who believe and have been forgiven. In Christ, we no longer deserve punishment, but instead we receive acceptance, blessing and love.

Declarations to Renew Your Mind: 1) God really loves me. He's absolutely crazy about me and wants nothing but the best for me. 2) God will show me the way to walk in life by demonstrating His goodness to me. 3) Jesus became a curse so that I wouldn't have to bear a curse. I get to walk in blessing, not punishment, because of what He has done.

Let's Just Laugh at This Lie
It's Hopeless

Laughable Assumptions Behind This Lie:
> ➤ This situation is impossible; there are no answers.
> ➤ I am destined for disappointment and unfulfilled promises.
> ➤ My unworthiness and wrong choices block all solutions coming to me.
> ➤ There are no such things as breakthroughs, successes or "suddenlies."
> ➤ I was born to fail for such a time as this.
> ➤ If I don't see God doing anything about this, it means He is not doing anything.

The Truth: Nothing is hopeless because all things are possible with God.
1) God called Abram the "father of a multitude," though he was 99 and had a barren wife. A year later, Sarah gave birth to Isaac (Genesis 17-21). 2) Joseph was hated by his brothers, thrown into a pit, sold into slavery, accused of rape, and sentenced to prison; yet he remained faithful and was promoted to the palace (Genesis 37-41). 3) Moses stood with a body of water before him, approaching enemies behind him, and complaining Israelites beside him; but he partnered with God to see the waters part and the Israelites experience freedom (Exodus 14). 4) The three Hebrew children miraculously survived the fiery furnace (Daniel 3). 5) Lazarus came to life after being dead four days (John 11).

Strategies for Overcoming This Lie:
1. **Take inventory of your hope** – Any thought in our mind that is not sparkling with confident hope indicates that it is under the influence of a lie (Romans 15:13). If you feel hopeless, ask the Holy Spirit to expose the lies that are being believed.
2. **Capture lies and hopeless thoughts** – Every thought that does not align with Christ, we have the authority to capture (2 Corinthians 10:5). What we think, we become (Proverbs 23:7). We can't afford to think anything that we do not want to become. Replace lies with God's truth to become free and to release freedom (John 8:32).
3. **Believe there is hope for every situation and every person** – He who possesses the highest levels of hope will have the highest levels of influence. 1 Corinthians 10:13 reveals that God has "the way" (hope) and an answer for every situation.

Declarations to Renew Your Mind: 1) Nothing is impossible with God. 2) The Holy Spirit lives inside of me, and He says nothing is hopeless. 3) All things work together for my good. 4) My heart and mind are glistening with confident hope, joy and expectation.

Let's Just Laugh at This Lie
I Will Always Be Sick

Laughable Assumptions Behind This Lie:
> ➤ Because I have not been perfect, I cannot expect to be healed.
> ➤ God is not capable or willing to heal a sickness like this.
> ➤ By His stripes, I was healed of everything except this disease.
> ➤ Jesus is running low on healing virtue.
> ➤ Jesus' death only paid for specific healings, and mine is not included.
> ➤ There is a specific lesson to be learned that will only come through enduring this sickness.
> ➤ Some sicknesses are supernaturally incurable.

The Truth: No sickness is too great to be healed. 1) A man with an infirmity for thirty-eight years was immediately healed (John 5:5-9). 2) Another man, blind from birth, completely regained his eyesight (John 9:1-8). 3) A paralytic carried by four men not only received forgiveness of sin, but his paralysis left, and he was fully restored (Mark 2:2-12). 4) A servant lying at home paralyzed and severely tormented was healed at the moment that Jesus declared healing (Matthew 8:5-13). 5) A man that was not only deaf, but also dumb, was instantaneously healed and could both hear and speak clearly (Mark 7:32-37).

Strategies for Overcoming This Lie:
1. **Recognize what is already yours** – "By whose stripes you <u>were</u> healed" (1 Peter 2:24). Realize this healing is past tense, therefore you have already been healed. Jesus cannot give you anything more to make you more healed. It is indeed finished.
2. **Refuse to be hopeless** – David spoke to his soul saying, "Why are you cast down, O my soul? And why are you disquieted within me? Hope in God, for I shall yet praise Him" (Psalm 42:5). It is important to not allow sickness to determine your level of hope (confident expectation).
3. **Increase in faith** – Meditate on God's promises; it will activate your faith. Put healing scriptures where you will see them (e.g. your car, mirror, refrigerator, wallet, screen saver, etc.). When you see them, speak them aloud. By hearing, faith increases (Romans 10:17). As you wait for your healing to manifest, don't be condemned if you need medicine or the help of doctors.

Declarations to Renew Your Mind: 1) The favor of God shields me, therefore sickness cannot touch me. 2) The same spirit that raised Jesus from the dead is giving life to my body right now (Romans 8:11). 3) My health is contagious. When I walk near sick people, they get healed.

Let's Just Laugh at This Lie
I Am Too Old to Make a Difference

Laughable Assumptions Behind This Lie:
- ➢ My best days are behind me.
- ➢ I don't have anything significant to contribute.
- ➢ There is nothing for me to do.
- ➢ My influence is declining.
- ➢ God primarily wants to use younger people.
- ➢ The younger generation will not receive from me.
- ➢ God's promises are more applicable to younger people.

The Truth: God regularly uses older people to do great things. The examples in scripture are many: 1) Abraham was 100 and Sarah 90 when their promise was fulfilled (Genesis 21). 2) Moses started his ministry at age 80. 3) Caleb was still overcoming at age 85. 4) Zacharias and Elizabeth had their main life purpose released in old age (Luke 1). 5) Jacob, just before his death, shaped the history of the nation of Israel by blessing his sons (Genesis 48). 6) Daniel was still powerfully influencing nations and political leaders in his final years (see book of Daniel).

Strategies for Overcoming This Lie:
1. **Believe that you have a future and a hope** – God is not done with you yet! There is a reason you are still here. God's thoughts toward you remain that you have a future and a hope (Jeremiah 29:11). Believe it.
2. **Realize you have a powerful impartation and blessing to give** – Joshua received wisdom because Moses laid his hands on him (Deuteronomy 34:9). We can release life-directing blessings to future generations (Genesis 48, 49). The laying on of hands is one of the elementary principles of Christian faith (Hebrews 6:1-3). Those who are older may not be able to work as hard as before, but they have something more important to do: impart and bless.
3. **Clarify your current assignment** – Something powerful happens when we clarify what we are called to do now. It may not be the same as before, but heaven will get behind us if we live purposefully. Whether you are called to be an encourager, blesser, intercessor, teacher, spiritual father/mother or something else; it is important for you to determine what your purpose and calling are now.

Declarations to Renew Your Mind: 1) My life is significant, and I have something important to do now. 2) I have a powerful blessing and impartation to give. 3) My best days are ahead of me.

Let's Just Laugh at This Lie
I Am Too Young To Make An Impact

Laughable Assumptions Behind This Lie:

> ➤ I have no influence because I am young.
> ➤ My prayers and words are not powerful or effective while I am young.
> ➤ If I were one year older, things would be different.
> ➤ A revival could never be started by a child or youth.
> ➤ Maturity and giftings are always on scale with your age.
> ➤ God looks at my age before He looks at my heart.
> ➤ It is easier to see miracles and to be used by God when you're older.

The Truth: God regularly and mightily uses the younger generation. 1) God did not agree with Jeremiah's self-assessment that he was too young to have a significant ministry (Jeremiah 1:6-7). 2) David, the youngest of all his brothers, was anointed king when he was a teenager (1 Samuel 16:11-13). 3) The apostle Paul instructs Timothy in 1 Timothy 4:12 to let no one look down on him because he is young, but to actually be an example. 4) Mary was a teenager when she gave birth to the Savior of the world (Luke 1:34-38). 5) A young boy's food was used by Jesus to feed 5,000 people (John 6:9-13). 6) Samuel was called by God to prophesy and minister before the Lord as a child (1 Samuel 2:18).

Strategies for Overcoming This Lie:

1. **Give God the little you have so that He has the opportunity to do great things** – Just as Jesus used the little boy with the five loaves and two fish, He can use you! God doesn't ask that you wait until you feel like you can offer a lot. He only asks that you offer what you have.

2. **Believe you are influencing those older than you by your lifestyle** – "Let no one despise your youth, but be an example to the believers in word, in conduct, in love, in spirit, in faith, in purity" (1 Timothy 4:12). Let your life speak louder than your words, and you will have influence.

3. **Align yourself under spiritual fathers and mothers who are being used by God** – Joshua had victory and wisdom largely because of his relationship with his spiritual father Moses (Deuteronomy 34:9 and Exodus 17:8-13). We, too, can accelerate our growth by honoring the key leaders in our lives.

Declarations to Renew Your Mind: 1) I am setting an example for others in word, conduct, love, spirit, faith and purity. 2) God is using me powerfully regardless of my age. 3) God provides wonderful spiritual fathers and mothers for my life.

Let's Just Laugh at This Lie
I Am a Failure

Laughable Assumptions Behind This Lie:

➢ God views me through the lens of my past mistakes.

➢ Others may recover from the kinds of mistakes I've made, but I cannot.

➢ If I fail, then it proves I am a failure as a person.

➢ I do not have what it takes to succeed.

➢ I have made this mistake too many times to be forgiven or to expect God's grace to help me.

➢ Every time I take one step forward, I take two steps backward.

➢ God may not have given up on others, but He has given up on me.

➢ Because of my past failures, I cannot have future significance.

The Truth: Past failures do not create your identity, nor do they disqualify you from having significant impact in the future. 1) Peter denied Christ three times, but was later restored to preach the message that birthed the church (Acts 2:14-41). 2) Moses failed at the start of his "ministry," but still became a great leader (Exodus 2:11-15; Exodus 14, 15). 3) Abraham failed when he and Hagar conceived Ishmael, but the nation of Israel still came from him (Genesis 16-21). 4) David committed adultery and murdered one of his own men; however, he repented and was recorded as one after God's heart (Acts 13:22). 5) Even Samson wreaked havoc for the enemy after miserably failing (Judges 16:25-30).

Strategies for Overcoming This Lie:

1. **Believe that God sees you through the lens of Jesus' death and resurrection** – "As far as the east is from the west, so far has He re-moved our transgressions from us" (Psalm 103:12). When we turn to God, He forgives us and rewrites our history!

2. **Overcome comparing yourself with others (2 Corinthians 10:12)** – Do not try to be someone else. Celebrate your own uniqueness and the personal calling you have from God. Be the best "you" that you can be.

3. **Trust that God uses all things to work for your good (Romans 8:28)** – When our hearts are turned toward Him, God even works our mis-takes into something powerful for our lives and the lives of others.

Declarations to Renew Your Mind: 1) I am successful, and I make a positive difference in the lives of those around me. 2) Everyday I succeed more and more at fulfilling God's purpose for my life. 3) God works my past failures into something glorious. 4) I am more than a conqueror in Christ Jesus.

Let's Just Laugh at This Lie
I Am Not Evangelistic

Laughable Assumptions Behind This Lie:

> ➢ My past experience determines who I really am.
> ➢ The Holy Spirit in me is not evangelistic.
> ➢ If I have not been evangelistic in the past, I can't be in the future.
> ➢ It is impossible for me to change and do what the Bible says I can do.
> ➢ My personality type has no avenues to reach others for Christ.
> ➢ My prayers for the lost are completely and totally ineffective.
> ➢ My past failure in evangelism means that I just need to give up trying to bring salvation to those who do not know Jesus.

The Truth: God brings salvation to others through various personalities and various methods. 1) Andrew invited someone to come to a place where they would meet Jesus (John 1:40-42). 2) Paul and Silas' praising God in a difficult time caused a jailer's whole family to be saved (Acts 16:23-34). 3) Peter's explanation of a supernatural "God phenomena" brought 3,000 into the kingdom (Acts 2:14-41). 4) Jesus spoke life to a woman by a well and gave her a word of knowledge. As a result, the woman brought many others to Him (John 4:39). 5) Philip was spiritually observant and asked a key question to a political leader, which resulted in him coming to salvation (Acts 8:26-39).

Strategies for Overcoming This Lie:

1. **Believe that you are evangelistic** – Paul told Timothy, "Do the work of an evangelist" (2 Timothy 4:5). The implication here is that Timothy's experience was non-evangelistic. In response to this, Paul basically says, "You are more evangelistic than you think. Arise and shine. Take steps to reach others for Christ. God will bless your efforts."

2. **Find your unique evangelistic style** – There is a distinctive way for you to reach others for Christ (i.e. friendship evangelism, power evangelism, presence evangelism, invitation evangelism, love evangelism, etc.). We are all to learn as many evangelistic methods as we can, but it is important to find our own style and enthusiastically walk in it.

3. **Keep prioritizing evangelism** – Feast on salvation testimonies, talk about souls being saved, emphasize water baptisms, read books, listen to CD's, attend evangelism seminars, learn evangelism techniques and do other things to impact your life to reach the lost.

Declarations to Renew Your Mind: 1) Many are born again because of my life. 2) I have a unique gifting to reach the lost for Christ. 3) Every day I influence people to come to Jesus.

Let's Just Laugh at This Lie
I Cannot Fulfill My Call Because of the People in My Life

Laughable Assumptions Behind This Lie:

➢ God is surprised and completely hindered by what the people in my life are doing. Their choices make it impossible for my calling to be fulfilled.

➢ The fulfillment of my calling is more determined by others than by me.

➢ What is happening in my life cannot possibly be used of God to give me even greater influence and ministry.

➢ I married the wrong person, and because of that, things are hopeless.

➢ If a relationship isn't instantly beneficial, it can't take me to my calling.

The Truth: Many godly ones have overcome difficult people. 1) David had a dad who did not believe in him, brothers who belittled him and a king who tried to kill him; but he still fulfilled his call (1 Samuel 16:10-13; 17:28; 24:1-2). 2) Joseph fulfilled his dream and destiny even though his brothers sold him into slavery, Potiphar's wife falsely accused him of rape and the chief butler forgot him (Genesis 37:23-24; 39:7-23; 40:23). 3) Jesus overcame dysfunctional disciples and a religious community that opposed Him. 4) Noah and his family were the only righteous people of his day, but he still fulfilled his calling (Genesis 6:13-22).

Strategies for Overcoming This Lie:

1. **Renew your beliefs about the people in your life** – Begin to believe that problematic people or relationships are actually opportunities to go higher in God.

2. **Believe in the power of His calling on your life** – God has an uncanny ability to cause us to fulfill our calling despite difficult people in our lives (see examples above). Even if we have made wrong relational choices, He will help us (as He did for Samson) to still make a tremendous spiritual difference (Judges 16:4-30).

3. **Understand that your response to the people in your life is more important than the people themselves** – The response to Jesus by the people in His hometown had a greater impact on their breakthrough than the fact that He was present. Rather than looking for new people in our lives, let's look for new mindsets about the people already in our lives. This does not mean we stay in abusive relationships, but it does mean we realize that we must get a plan to increasingly see people as God sees them.

Declarations to Renew Your Mind: 1) I see people in my life as strategic opportunities, not obstacles. 2) I have renewed mindsets about my calling and the people in my life. 3) Daily, I am making progress and stepping into my calling.

Let's Just Laugh at This Lie
Good Works Are the Requirement to Go to Heaven

Laughable Assumptions Behind This Lie:

> Believing in Jesus and being born again are not necessary to be saved.

> John 3:16 is not true when it says that "whoever believes in Him should not perish but have everlasting life." God meant to say, "Whoever behaves better than most shall not perish, but have everlasting life."

> Jesus' death on the cross was unnecessary because people go to heaven just by being good anyway.

> Just as all roads can lead to San Francisco, all religions lead to heaven.

> The books of Galatians and Romans are lying when they say that faith in Christ, not good works, is the pathway to salvation and heaven.

> There's no need for a New Testament of grace and faith because God can't dislodge Himself from the Old Testament based on law and works.

The Truth: True faith in Christ saves, not good works. 1) "For by grace you have been saved through faith, and that not of yourselves; *it is* the gift of God, not of works, lest anyone should boast" (Ephesians 2:8-9). 2) "Therefore, having been justified by faith, we have peace with God through our Lord Jesus Christ" (Romans 5:1). 3) "That if you confess with your mouth the Lord Jesus and believe in your heart that God has raised Him from the dead, you will be saved" (Romans 10:9). 4) "Nevertheless knowing that a man is not justified by the works of the law, but through faith in Christ Jesus" (Galatians 2:16).

Strategies for Overcoming This Lie:

1. **Immerse yourself in the epistles (Romans through Jude)** – Gorge on Paul's writings—especially Galatians and Romans. Ask God for revelation about saving faith.

2. **Answer this question from God accurately** – "Why should I let you into My heaven?" The only acceptable answer according to the Bible is "You should let me into Your heaven because of what Jesus did for me. His death and resurrection have given me the way to be with You for eternity. I believe!" Any answer focusing on good works disqualifies us.

3. **Commit yourself to reaching others with the gospel** – As we give evangelism a main priority in our lives, it reinforces the basic truths of Christianity and helps us stay on track in our core beliefs.

Declarations to Renew Your Mind: 1) I am saved through faith, not works. 2) Good works result from good beliefs, and I have sound doctrinal beliefs. 3) Revelation about the greatness of Christ's death and resurrection is exploding in me.

Let's Just Laugh at This Lie
I Am Not Worthy to Be Blessed

Laughable Assumptions Behind This Lie:
- ➤ I might have been saved by grace, but I'm blessed based on my works.
- ➤ God's primary concern is how I perform.
- ➤ If I behave a little better than the average Christian, I will be blessed.
- ➤ I've messed up too many times to be blessed.
- ➤ There are people more worthy of God's blessing than me.
- ➤ God will have to discipline me before I can be blessed.
- ➤ God can't bless me until I am perfect.
- ➤ God can't trust me with His blessings.

The Truth: Jesus has made believers worthy to be blessed. 1) Abraham, our example of faith, believed and it was "accounted to him as righteousness." His faith in God's promises caused a blessing for him that was not dependent on works (Galatians 3:6). 2) "David also describes the blessedness of the man to whom God imputes righteousness apart from works: *'Blessed are those whose lawless deeds are forgiven, And whose sins are covered; Blessed is the man to whom the LORD shall not impute sin'*" Romans 4:6-8). 3) Jesus took the curse we deserved so we could walk in the blessing He deserved (Galatians 3:13-14).

Strategies for Overcoming This Lie:
1. **Find your identity as God's precious child** – God has adopted you into His family (Ephesians 1:5, Galatians 4:4-6), and you are His beloved. He is a good Father who only wants the best for you (Luke 11:11-13). Your position as His child declares you are worthy!
2. **Realize that it's not about you—it's about Him!** – As we were sinners in Adam's sin (not our own), we are righteous in Christ's righteousness, not ours (Romans 5:17-19). You are crucified with Christ and it is no longer you that lives, but Him, and He is very worthy (Galatians 2:20).
3. **Start expecting blessing to follow you** – Favor marks your life as His son or daughter. We don't have to chase opportunities, finances, health, good relationships or any blessing—they are supernaturally attracted to the favor upon our lives! Joseph was constantly put in dire situations, but God's favor marked him to rise to the top in every one of them (Genesis 39-41).

Declarations to Renew Your Mind: 1) I am a beloved child of God, and He delights in giving me good things. 2) When God looks at me He sees the righteousness of Jesus Christ! 3) I am blessed in everything I do; the goodness of God gravitates towards me.

Let's Just Laugh at This Lie
I Am Who My Experience Says I Am

Laughable Assumptions Behind This Lie:
> ➢ My past determines my identity, not God's Word.
> ➢ Because of my repeated failures, I am not who God says I am.
> ➢ What I have experienced cancels God's promises about me.
> ➢ It is my nature to sin as a Christian.
> ➢ . God has overestimated me.
> ➢ I live by sight, not by faith.
> ➢ God's prophetic words over my life must be wrong.

The Truth: I am who God says I am, not who my experience says I am.
1) God called Abraham the father of many nations before he had any children (Genesis 17). 2) God said Gideon was a great leader when Gideon thought he was the weakest of the weak (Judges 6:11-16). 3) Moses was unconfident and stuttering but was told he was the deliverer of Israel (Exodus 3, 4). 4) Joseph was a great leader in God's view even when imprisoned (Genesis 39, 40). 5) Jesus called Peter a rock and planned to build His church through him, even though Peter would deny Him three times (Matthew 16:18). 6) David was anointed king while living in the experience of a shepherd (1 Samuel 16:13).

Strategies for Overcoming This Lie:
1. **Look at life from God's perspective** – Man tends to make conclusions by looking at outward appearances that result from past experiences, but God has a much higher perspective (1 Samuel 16:7, Isaiah 55:8,9). We are called to look at life (especially our own) through God's beliefs.
2. **Call forth those things in your life that do not exist as though they do (Romans 4:17)** – This is God's way of bringing life to dead areas of our lives. Romans 4 reveals Abraham's journey of breaking his agreement (or understanding) with his experience, and agreeing with God. One of the main ways he accomplished this was to call himself who he was "before he was."
3. **Surround yourself with encouraging people** – In order to be filled with hope and encouragement, surround yourself with people like Joshua, Caleb and Barnabas. As part of your plan for this encouragement, feast on teachings that build hope in this truth: *I am not who my experience says I am, but I am who God says I am.*

Declarations to Renew Your Mind: 1) I am who God says I am, not who my experience says I am. 2) My righteousness is sealed in the finished work of Christ. 3) My experience is transformed as I believe the truth of who I truly am.

Let's Just Laugh at This Lie
The Greatest Christians Are Those with Public Ministries

Laughable Assumptions Behind This Lie:

➤ Those without high profile ministries are substandard Christians.

➤ Heaven's best places are reserved for speakers and worship leaders.

➤ 1 Corinthians 13 love is unimportant as long as I am doing great outward things that are well-known.

➤ All Christians should first seek to have a famous ministry.

➤ Those who are not confident and skilled to do public ministry should feel depressed about their lives.

➤ Things done in secret slip through the cracks and will not be rewarded.

➤ King David only became a great person once he killed Goliath.

➤ God is not interested in raising up leaders in business, education or any sphere other than the church.

The Truth: Most of the greatest ministries are not public ministries. Here are some examples: 1) Prayer (1 Timothy 2:1-4). 2) Encouragement (Hebrews 10:23-25). 3) Love (1 Corinthians 13). 4) Generosity (Romans 12:8). 5) Evangelism (Acts 8:26-38). 6) Mentoring and discipling (2 Timothy 2:2). 7) Commitment to your family (Ephesians 5:21-6:3). 8) Being an armor bearer for a leader (1 Samuel 14). 9) Administration and helps (1 Corinthians 12:28).

Strategies for Overcoming This Lie:

1. **Realize that people don't have great ministries by trying to have a great ministry, but by having great beliefs and great priorities** – We turn into a leader because God's grace has brought transformation in us. The truths and experiences that result from this make us a spiritual father or mother, regardless of whether it is expressed publicly or not.

2. **Decide to do small things in a great way** – Whatever is done for Jesus in faith has significance. We do not need to be known by the masses to powerfully impact the world.

3. **Honor those who serve behind the scenes in the body of Christ** – Celebrate those with the gift of helps. Honor those who are called to prayer. Do cartwheels for those who serve as ushers, visit the sick, go to the prisons, practice hospitality, comfort the hurting, give sacrificially or serve in other seemingly unspectacular ways.

Declarations to Renew Your Mind: 1) I am a significant part of the body of Christ. 2) I honor those with public ministries, but I also honor those who minister behind the scenes. 3) I am a person who has great beliefs and great priorities.

Let's Just Laugh at This Lie
I Am a Disorganized Person

Laughable Assumptions Behind This Lie:

- ➤ The Bible says that I have a sound mind, but that does not include the ability to have order in my life.
- ➤ If I regularly say, "I am disorganized" or "I am non-administrative," it will have nothing to do with what I experience in those areas of my life.
- ➤ The gift of administration only hinders kingdom advancement.
- ➤ Because the rapture is coming soon, I should not plan or organize.
- ➤ The renewing of the mind will not affect a person's level of organization.
- ➤ Only the unspiritual would regularly set aside time to organize and plan.
- ➤ God prefers to work through spontaneous people.
- ➤ I'm just too busy to be organized.

The Truth: Strong influencers order their lives to accomplish great things, and we are made to greatly influence others. 1) God is a God of order, and we are made in His image (Genesis 1:27). He planned well for creation, for our salvation, for Solomon's temple and for many other things in scripture. 2) Noah followed a plan to build the ark, even though it took him one hundred years to do so (Genesis 6:14-22). 3) Jesus was very purposeful in what He did (and what He did not do) so that He could fully bring about God's redemption. 4) The Apostle Paul was systematic in how he presented the gospel in the epistles.

Strategies for Overcoming This Lie:

1. **Believe you have a sound mind and the mind of Christ** – "God has . . . given us . . . <u>a sound mind</u>" (2 Timothy 1:7). "We have the mind of Christ" (1 Corinthians 2:16). God's power is not just for healing and miracles but is also for the supernatural organizing of resources, people and time to do extraordinary things for Him.

2. **Prioritize planning and creating structures to sustain personal and corporate revival** – Regularly invest in and improve your skills of time management, people management, basic administration, goal setting and other aspects of successful organizing.

3. **Celebrate your improvement, not just perfection** – Just as a toddler doesn't physically walk well when he first starts, neither will we become instantly organized when we first try. Just stick with it. Celebrate small improvements, and don't let failure stop you from trying again.

Declarations to Renew Your Mind: 1) I organize my time and resources well to accomplish things for Christ. 2) I am both spontaneous and organized. 3) I plan well for the future.

Let's Just Laugh at This Lie

In Bad Economic Times, It is Unwise to Have Children

Laughable Assumptions Behind This Lie:

- ➤ In times of economic recession, God's resources are limited.
- ➤ If we have children during a bad economic time, God will consider us irresponsible and remove His blessing from us.
- ➤ God is regretting telling us to "be fruitful and multiply," as He did not foresee the recession.
- ➤ Children are a heritage from the Lord, but only if planned correctly.
- ➤ God tolerates us having children but does not get excited about it.
- ➤ God much prefers testimonies of heathens getting saved than the testimonies of those who were raised in Christian homes.
- ➤ When an unplanned baby is born, God and the angels worry about whether or not there will be enough provision available for the newborn.
- ➤ No great people have ever been born during economically bad times.

The Truth: God's biggest solutions start with a baby being born (often in less than ideal situations). 1) Moses was born at a time when it was unwise for Hebrew women to have children (Exodus 1, 2). 2) Samuel entered the world in a spiritually dark time (1 Samuel 3:1). 3) Isaac and John the Baptist both had parents who were very old (Genesis 21; Luke 1). 4) Jesus was born into a situation where there were rumors of Him being an illegitimate child (Matthew 1:18-20).

Strategies for Overcoming This Lie:

1. **Believe children are a blessing from the Lord** – "Behold, children *are* a heritage from the LORD, the fruit of the womb *is* a reward. Like arrows in the hand of a warrior, so *are* the children of one's youth. Happy *is* the man who has his quiver full of them" (Psalm 127:3-5).

2. **Realize the Christian family is God's #1 plan for evangelism and kingdom advancement** – "Be fruitful and multiply; fill the earth . . ." (Genesis 1:28). This first command in the Bible is still God's heart for His people. Yes, it is good for a couple to prepare in lifestyle and finances before having children, but none can fully prepare for parenting.

3. **Know God will provide for your family** – When we dedicate our lives and children to the Lord, we take a main step in kingdom advancement. Whether our child is planned or unplanned, we can claim Matthew 6:33's promise of provision as we "seek first His kingdom."

Declarations to Renew Your Mind: 1) Children are a blessing from the Lord. 2) God supernaturally provides for the needs of my family and children. 3) God loves families and children.

Let's Just Laugh at This Lie
I Will Never Lose This Weight

Laughable Assumptions Behind This Lie:

- ➢ God has no solutions for my weight problem.
- ➢ If I just look at food, I will put on weight.
- ➢ Jesus can raise the dead, but He doesn't care about my weight.
- ➢ Older people's metabolism make it impossible not to put on weight.
- ➢ Even if there were solutions, I could not implement them because there is something extraordinarily and uniquely wrong with me.
- ➢ No one in the history of mankind with my weight problem and my temperament has ever significantly lost weight and kept it off.
- ➢ God is frustrated with me about this and does not want to help me.
- ➢ The promise "all things are possible" does not include my losing weight.

The Truth: God has solutions for long-standing, persistent problems (1 Corinthians 10:13). 1) A man with a thirty-eight year infirmity was healed (John 5:1-15). 2) A man lame from birth was transformed through Peter and John (Acts 3:1-10). 3) A woman received a miraculous healing for a serious and lingering problem by touching Jesus (Luke 8:40-48). 4) A boy was delivered of the habit of throwing himself in the fire (Mark 9:21-27).

Strategies for Overcoming This Lie:

1. **Develop a plan to build hope in your life** – Hopelessness about the weight issue is a bigger problem than the weight issue. There are no hopeless situations, only hopeless people. Once people get true hope, the circumstance cannot stay the same. Find ways to feed your hope.

2. **Shake off condemnation and come boldly to the throne of grace** – "For we do not have a High Priest who cannot sympathize with our weaknesses . . . come boldly to the throne of grace, that we may obtain mercy and find grace to help in time of need" (Hebrews 4:15-16). The feelings of condemnation are also a bigger problem than the extra pounds.

3. **Bridle your tongue** – James 3:2 says that our bodies can be controlled if we bridle our words. One of the greatest things you can do is speak life over your body and over your physical wellbeing.

4. **Keep knocking on the door of physical wellbeing** – Don't give up. Keep trying new ways. You will find the key for your situation.

Declarations to Renew Your Mind: 1) I am a fat burning machine that is at the perfect weight. 2) I love to exercise, eat right and drink lots of water. 3) I have divine strategies and power to be the right weight.

Let's Just Laugh at This Lie
My Life is Ruined by That Decision I Made

Laughable Assumptions Behind This Lie:

➤ My past defines my future.

➤ Even God cannot redeem this one.

➤ My sin is more powerful than the promises of God.

➤ There is completely and utterly no hope for me.

➤ My past actions are more powerful than my current beliefs.

➤ No one could be restored from this bad decision.

➤ Things will never change.

➤ God only uses people who have not messed up.

The Truth: God can redeem anything, *especially* my situation. 1) God used Samson mightily after his major backsliding (Judges 16). 2) Saul (Paul) wrote a good portion of the New Testament after persecuting Christians for a living. 3) God redeemed David's adultery and murder by bringing forth Solomon (2 Samuel 12:24). 4) Peter is used powerfully throughout Acts after denying Christ three times. 5) The demon-possessed man of the Gadarenes was transformed into an evangelist to his city (Mark 5:20). 6) Jonah ran from God's call but later brought revival to Nineveh (see book of Jonah).

Strategies for Overcoming This Lie:

1. **Pursue breakthrough in the very area you failed** – Often it is the area of our greatest struggle where we obtain the biggest victories in life (and where we will have the most influence). Get excited about how God is going to help you overcome in this part of your life!

2. **Remember the power of Jesus' blood** – When we were covered by the blood of Jesus, it was strong enough to cleanse us of all our past, present and future sins. Nothing is too bad or too strong for the redemptive power of His blood (Ephesians 1:7).

3. **Declare and envision future victories** – If we can have vision for our future (personal hope based on the goodness and promises of God), we can have power for the present. As we align our beliefs with God's plan for our redemption, it unlocks powerful breakthrough in our lives.

Declarations to Renew Your Mind: 1) I live from Christ's victory, not my own. 2) Every poor decision in my life is being redeemed right now into a greater victory. 3) I am filled with glistening hope!

Let's Just Laugh at This Lie
I Cannot Change

Laughable Assumptions Behind This Lie:
> God's transforming power of restoration and redemption is not strong enough to cause me to change.
> The renewing of the mind does not transform people like me.
> It is easier for other people to change than it is for me.
> Change is easier for the younger generation.
> My personality is particularly stubborn and resistant to change.
> It is too late for me to change so I should just settle for life as it is.
> If I try to change, it will not work, and I will actually lose ground.

The Truth: Positive change is possible for every type of person. 1) Saul, after killing Christians, became one of the strongest Christian influencers ever through one God encounter (Acts 9). 2) The severely demon-possessed man of the Gadarenes was delivered and immediately commissioned as a missionary (Mark 5:1-20). 3) David's "mighty men" were once unqualified misfits (1 Samuel 22:1-2; 2 Samuel 23). 4) Mary Magdalene was freed from seven demons to become a powerful follower of Jesus (Luke 8:2). 5) The entire city of Ninevah turned from wickedness to full repentance and revival in one day (Jonah 3:5-10).

Strategies for Overcoming This Lie:
1. **Increase your hope** – The belief that we cannot change is actually a bigger problem than any particular negative habit or situation we face. The New Covenant believer is to focus much more on beliefs than conduct (Galatians 3:1-5). Transformed behavior results from the intentional renewing of our minds with truth (Romans 12:2).
2. **Give yourself time to change** – When a farmer plants his crop, he does not wake up early the next morning to check the soil, and then become discouraged with the lack of progress. Transformation is a process of moving from "glory to glory" that not only results from changing what we believe, but from being intimate with God (2 Corinthians 3:18).
3. **Never stop starting** – "And let us not grow weary while doing good, for in due season we shall reap if we do not lose heart" (Galatians 6:9). Never give up! Never give up! Never give up! If you fall down, get up again. If one thing did not work, try another. God has 100 ideas for how change can happen (James 1:5).

Declarations to Renew Your Mind: 1) It is easy for me to change. 2) My intimacy with Christ brings about transformation. 3) I am daily being made to look more like Christ. 4) I get excited when I find an area in my life that needs change. 5) My hope is increasing.

Let's Just Laugh at This Lie

A Curse is More Powerful Than a Blessing

Laughable Assumptions Behind This Lie:

➤ Darkness is more powerful than light.

➤ Though Satan is defeated, his curses are still victorious.

➤ Generational curses are more powerful than generational blessings.

➤ If we are cursed, we should worry about bad coming to us; but if we are blessed, we should not expect outrageously good things to come to us.

➤ A spoken blessing isn't really powerful; it's just a courtesy gesture when someone sneezes.

➤ Christ's work on the cross is easily overturned by a curse.

The Truth: Christians are delivered from curses and are blessed. 1) Just as Jesus took our sins, He also took our curses and offers blessing in exchange. "Christ has redeemed us from the curse of the law, having become a curse for us . . . that the blessing of Abraham might come upon the Gentiles in Christ Jesus" (Galatians 3:13-14). 2) We have authority over the curse giver. "Behold, I give you the authority . . . over all the power of the enemy" (Luke 10:19). 3) A blessing is more powerful than a curse (just as light is more powerful than darkness). The Patriarchs blessed their descendents and history is still affected. "By faith Isaac blessed Jacob and Esau concerning things to come. By faith Jacob . . . blessed each of the sons of Joseph" (Hebrews 11:20-21).

Strategies for Overcoming This Lie:

1. **Gorge on truth about the greatness of our salvation** – It is bigger than we know. Satan's defeat was more conclusive than has ever been understood. When Jesus said, "It is finished," He could have just as well said, "The devil is finished." All that is left for us to do is to believe Colossians 2:15—"Having disarmed principalities and powers, He made a public spectacle of them, triumphing over them in it."

2. **Receive every blessing by faith** – Intentionally "worry" with God about the good that will overtake you after Christians bless you.

3. **Build confidence in your spiritual authority** – "Resist the devil and he will flee from you" (James 4:7). There is a lifestyle available that is fearless concerning the devil. Obviously, we don't want to be foolish or naive concerning the demonic, but we don't need to be afraid either.

Declarations to Renew Your Mind: 1) Light is more powerful than darkness. 2) Blessings are much stronger than curses. 3) The blessings that have been pronounced over me protect me from any curses in my environment.

Let's Just Laugh at This Lie
That Relationship Can Never Be Healed or Restored

Laughable Assumptions Behind This Lie:

- ➤ Miscommunication and broken relationships follow me everywhere I go.
- ➤ I will need to do everything perfectly to have this relationship restored. It is all up to me. God has not and will not do anything about it.
- ➤ God only cares that my ministry is successful, not my relationships.
- ➤ All things are possible, but restoring this relationship is not.
- ➤ Restoration hinges upon the other person's willingness to change.
- ➤ Relationship restoration is not included in our salvation.
- ➤ Because there is something uniquely wrong with me, and because I am so unworthy, this relationship cannot be restored.

The Truth: Restoration is possible for any relationship. 1) Paul was restored with Christians after he had greatly alienated himself by killing and persecuting them (Acts 9:26-28). 2) Paul and Mark were restored to one another after Paul had deemed Mark unfit to minister with him (Acts 15:37-41, Colossians 4:10). 3) Joseph was restored to his brothers even though they had sold him into slavery (Genesis 45:4-16). 4) Jacob and Esau had their heart connection healed after Esau had despised Jacob for twenty years and had wanted him dead (Genesis 27:41; Genesis 33:4). 5) Peter was restored to Jesus after denying Him three times (John 21:15-17).

Strategies for Overcoming This Lie:

1. **Prioritize healthy relationships** – Doing what we can to keep peace with others is so vital that God says if we enter into worship and are at odds with someone else, we should stop immediately, make amends, and then return to worship (Matthew 5:23-24). We are to do all that is possible on our part to live at peace with everyone (Romans 12:18).

2. **Repent for our faults** – Take responsibility for any of your wrongdoings and ask the other person to forgive you (Matthew 7:5). Defenses crumble when we become vulnerable with our faults.

3. **Choose to Forgive** – Forgive the other person for any wrong or hurt that he or she caused. Forgiveness is not a feeling; it's a choice. It voids all debts and resets the standard (Colossians 3:13). Note: We can walk in forgiveness and still have healthy boundaries in relationships.

Declarations to Renew Your Mind: 1) I walk in forgiveness toward everyone I know. 2) Peace reigns in my relationship with _____. 3) All of my relationships are healthy, full of life and bursting with joy.

Let's Just Laugh at This Lie
I Don't Have Any Influence in This Place

Laughable Assumptions Behind This Lie:

- ➤ I am a victim to the perceptions that other people have of me.
- ➤ I should not expect to have influence or favor in my home or local area.
- ➤ I don't influence the spiritual atmosphere in this place because greater is he that is in the world, than He that is in me.
- ➤ I am tolerated but not celebrated.
- ➤ Because I struggle communicating, I don't have influence.
- ➤ I have been given dominion over all the earth, except this place.
- ➤ God has given us everywhere the sole of our feet tread, but my feet must be defective or something.
- ➤ If I don't see anything happening, it means nothing is happening.

The Truth: Our favor and influence will grow as we consistently renew our minds with truth. 1) Joseph demonstrated an excellent spirit in prison which caused him to be promoted to an unbelievable position of authority in Egypt (Genesis 41:38-45). 2) Daniel prospered inwardly during dark years for Israel; and as a result, he greatly influenced ungodly kings and nations—and wrote a book that was chosen by God to be in the Bible. 3) Paul stayed on the ship (both physically and in his attitude) after his good counsel was rejected, and he became the key influencer in a future crisis (Acts 27). 4) The unlearned disciples went from having little influence to turning the world upside down because they were "with Jesus" (Acts 4:13; 17:6).

Strategies for Overcoming This Lie:

1. **Celebrate the favor and influence you already have** – Nobody is valued as much as they want to be, but we each have influence with important people and situations. If we steward this well and are thankful for the favor we have, more will come.

2. **Believe you walk in increasing favor and influence because Christ lives in you** – Jesus "increased . . . in favor with God and men" (Luke 2:52), and so will we as we understand who we are in Him.

3. **Win people to yourself first and then to your words** – "[Unbelieving husbands], without a word, may be won by the conduct of their wives" (1 Peter 3:1). Instead of begging God to change people's behavior, live in such a way that will capture their hearts.

Declarations to Renew Your Mind: 1) I am increasing in favor with God and man. 2) My influence is increasing. 3) My current soul prosperity is leading to increasing future influence.

Let's Just Laugh at This Lie
I Am Always Stressed in Airports and Traffic Jams

Laughable Assumptions Behind This Lie:

> ➤ I am hard wired to be tense and grouchy in airports and traffic jams.
>
> ➤ God understands that I will have a sour disposition in these situations, so He waits for these events to be over to speak with me.
>
> ➤ If Jesus were living on earth today, He too would be uptight in airports and would have road rage in heavy traffic.
>
> ➤ It's impossible to not be controlled by the negative emotions around me.
>
> ➤ If I am late or miss my flight, God has no solutions, nor can He work things for good.
>
> ➤ There is no divine purpose or opportunity in a stressed-out airport or traffic jam. It is always an attack of the devil to be resisted.

The Truth: There is unique grace available for every kind of situation we face. 1) There is grace to worship and praise. Silas and Paul's praise created a revival in a dreadful, stress-filled prison (Acts 16:16-34). 2) There is grace that provides strength. "My grace is sufficient for you, for My strength is made perfect in weakness" (2 Corinthians 12:9). Paul received this promise when facing an ongoing frustration. 3) There is a delivering grace that increasingly manifests as we walk in peace. "Then passing through the midst of [those wanting to kill Him], He went His way" (Luke 4:30).

Strategies for Overcoming This Lie:

1. **Realize this is an opportunity to build your peace "muscle"** – "And the God of peace will crush Satan under your feet shortly" (Romans 16:20). Jesus slept during a storm and then got up to rebuke it (Mark 4:35-41). Stressful situations create an opportunity to access higher levels of peace that will give us greater authority over the storms of life.

2. **Increase your time management skills, but let go of perfectionism so you can enjoy the journey** – Much stress can be reduced by giving yourself extra time when traveling. Even so, nobody will always plan properly or be able to avoid unforeseen events—so purpose to be more joyful when things aren't going well. Others will be glad you did.

3. **Look for the divine purpose in the situation** – Open your eyes to the opportunities all around you. Is there someone to minister to? Is there something else to do? Turn the stress into something positive.

Declarations to Renew Your Mind: 1) My peace is growing, and it is a great spiritual weapon. 2) I laugh a lot in airports and traffic jams. 3) I find divine purpose in inconvenient and stressful moments.

Let's Just Laugh at This Lie
If I Am Not Popular, I Am Insignificant and a Failure

Laughable Assumptions Behind This Lie:
- ➤ Being popular and considered cool by other people is the most important thing in life.
- ➤ What people think of me is more important than what God thinks of me.
- ➤ No one else ever feels alone or insecure but me.
- ➤ Peer popularity is the highest level of success.
- ➤ Anyone that has ever been successful has never been disliked.
- ➤ Feeling disliked and unpopular is a sure sign of failure and defeat.
- ➤ Seek ye first popularity, and all good things will be added unto you.
- ➤ Jesus' main goal when here on earth was to be liked and popular, so that should be our goal, too.

The Truth: Popularity is fleeting, but favor and respect create lasting influence. 1) Respect comes by standing for something – For 70 years Daniel stood for God with integrity and truth. He made a long-term difference in godless nations. Some hated him, but when trouble came, he was the first to be called. 2) Respect comes from not following the crowd – Joseph chose a higher path by dreaming big about his future, walking in sexual purity, excelling in prison and forgiving others. As a result, he had great favor and influence. 3) Respect comes from valuing ourselves – Jesus said, "Love your neighbor as yourself" (Mark 12:31). Truly loving ourselves frees us from being addicted to the praise of man.

Strategies for Overcoming This Lie:
1. **Believe you are uniquely and wonderfully made** – God created you to be a one of a kind blessing to the world. No two people carry the same characteristics or assignment in life. We have something that only we can do and be. Each of us is important!
2. **Overcome being a people pleaser and be willing to be different** – Those who live for the approval of others will have a miserable existence. People pleasers aren't respected anyway, so it is pointless to continually try to make others like us. Those who live by strong core values (that honor God) will be respected much more in the long run.
3. **Have a heart for those who are unpopular** – Love the popular (and learn not to be intimidated by them), but be a friend to those who need one. Become the biggest encourager you know.

Declarations to Renew Your Mind: 1) I am secure in who I am. 2) People respect me because of my strong convictions and core values. 3) God's approval of me causes me to live an abundant life.

Let's Just Laugh at This Lie
Because I Don't Shake or Fall Down, God Must Not be Touching Me

Laughable Assumptions Behind This Lie:
- Nothing can happen on the inside of me unless it is clear that something is happening on the outside.
- God has ordained only one way for people to respond to His Spirit; and because I don't respond that way, He is frustrated with me.
- If I am not having regular manifestations of the Spirit in my life, then I am obviously an inferior Christian with huge, unresolved issues.
- We are to eagerly desire physical manifestations, especially shaking.
- These signs shall follow those who believe: shaking, falling down and yelling loudly.

The Truth: As we believe that God is touching us (whether we feel it or not), we will have life changing encounters with Him. 1) In John 20:22 Jesus breathed on the disciples and told them, "Receive the Holy Spirit." He did not force the Spirit on them but called them to "receive" by faith. 2) In Mark 11:24 Jesus said, "Whatever things you ask when you pray, believe that you receive *them,* and you will have *them.*" 3) Luke 11:13 invites us to ask for Holy Spirit encounters. "If you then, being evil, know how to give good gifts to your children, how much more will *your* heavenly Father give the Holy Spirit to those who ask Him!" God would not have us ask for something that we could not have.

Strategies for Overcoming This Lie:
1. **Overcome the "There is something uniquely wrong with me" syndrome** – Of course there's something wrong with you because there is something wrong with everyone. That's why God sent Jesus. Get over it! Excessive introspection won't help. Relax and receive by faith.
2. **Let go of control and fear, and "lean into" what God is doing** – Some say, "I am not going to let anyone push me down when they pray for me. It has to be God!" This sounds noble, but it's likely to hinder us.
3. **Focus on Jesus, not physical manifestations** – When Peter walked on water, he only began to sink when he focused on the physical things around him instead of Jesus. When we spend time with Jesus, things will begin to happen; but they should not become our focus, pursuit or gauge of spirituality.

Declarations to Renew Your Mind: 1) I have healthy attitudes about spiritual encounters. 2) I have learned to receive by faith, and my encounters are increasing as a result. 3) I am very free in God.

Let's Just Laugh at This Lie
I Am Not Spiritual Enough to Be Used by God

Laughable Assumptions Behind This Lie:

- ➤ God is frustrated with me because I am not spiritual enough.
- ➤ Everyone who is used by God is more spiritual than me.
- ➤ Because I don't pray for five hours per day and fast extensively, God considers me unspiritual and will not move through me.
- ➤ I need to wear camel's hair and eat locusts and wild honey if I truly want to have influence.
- ➤ I haven't had visions or seen angels, so I cannot be effective spiritually.
- ➤ Because I am busy and have responsibilities, my life is not spiritual.
- ➤ If only I could die more to myself, then God could really use me.

The Truth: Although we should desire and seek God for supernatural encounters, we also need to remember that God uses seemingly ordinary people to do extraordinary things. 1) Mary and Joseph were common people who were not overly spiritual, but they were chosen by God to be the parents of Jesus Christ (Luke 1:26-33). 2) Ananias wasn't listed as one who was super spiritual, yet God spoke to him in a vision to go and lay hands on Saul to restore his sight (Acts 9:10-12). 3) Peter and John were average men whose "being with Jesus" caused them to be anointed to preach the gospel and perform extraordinary miracles (Acts 4:13).

Strategies for Overcoming This Lie:

1. **Know that Jesus has qualified you to be used by God** – We are made acceptable to God completely through the blood of Christ (Romans 5:1). We don't receive from God by works but by "the hearing of faith" (Galatians 3:1-5). Let's hear who we are in Christ and what Christ has done for us, and we will be used of God in mighty ways.

2. **Know that God has given you a unique anointing and calling, and you do not need to compare yourself with others** – Believe that you play an important role in God's plan for the world and the church (1 Corinthians 12:4-7). Certainly we don't just settle for our current level of experience, but we do need to believe we are spiritually "hard-wired" with a distinctive temperament to do great things (Romans 12:4-8).

3. **Expect an increase of spiritual encounters in your life** – If we believe it, we will receive it (Matthew 21:22).

Declarations to Renew Your Mind: 1) I am a spiritual person because the Holy Spirit lives within me. 2) I am a supernatural conduit of the Holy Spirit. 3) I am becoming more like Christ daily.

Let's Just Laugh at This Lie
Higher Levels in God Attract Higher Problem-Causing Devils

Laughable Assumptions Behind This Lie:
> We are to expect a life of growing difficulty as we spiritually advance.
> Church leaders have miserable lives because of spiritual attacks.
> Generals are the least protected in an army.
> Unless I am experiencing an attack, I must not be a threat to the devil.
> The safest thing to do is to not advance spiritually in Christ.
> The very spiritual person will talk more about Satan's ability to attack than God's ability to protect.
> Our expectations have nothing to do with what we will experience.

The Truth: God supernaturally protects those on the front lines. 1) Daniel, a front line leader, was protected in the lion's den (Daniel 6). 2) The three Hebrew children (who were advancing young zealots) were kept safe in the fiery furnace (Daniel 3). 3) Jesus walked through a multitude that wanted to kill Him (Luke 4:28-30). 4) Psalm 91 speaks of high-level protection for those that are pressing into the deep things of God.

Strategies for Overcoming This Lie:
1. **Realize Jesus is our example of walking in higher protection** – His life reveals what is possible. He is to be our example, not Job or others. Remember, His crucifixion resulted from His choosing to die for us, not a breaking down of spiritual protection over Him.

2. **Believe that kingdom advancement will increase the manifestation of blessing and protection** – "I exhort . . . that . . . prayers . . . be made for all men, for kings and all who are in authority, that we may lead a quiet and peaceable life . . . For this *is* good and acceptable in the sight of God our Savior, who desires all men to be saved and to come to the knowledge of the truth" (1 Timothy 2:1-4).

3. **Talk about and expect God's increasing protection as we advance spiritually** – Yes, we realize that there will be martyrs and those who suffer in the advancement of the gospel, but we must reject beliefs that will attract unnecessary pain and difficulty into our lives (and that will subconsciously cause us to not want to advance spiritually).

Declarations to Renew Your Mind: 1) As I move forward in God, I have increasing strength and protection. 2) God's protection is a greater reality than Satan's attacks. 3) God's generals are the most protected in battle.

Let's Just Laugh at This Lie
Because I Don't Have a High Paying Job, I am a Failure

Laughable Assumptions Behind This Lie:

- ➢ My value in life is determined by how high my salary is.
- ➢ God uses the same measurement for success as the world.
- ➢ The most important question to ask when choosing a career or a place of employment is "How much money will I make?"
- ➢ God prefers rich people because their tithes are bigger.
- ➢ The story of the widow who gave two mites is a mistranslation—she actually gave $20,000.
- ➢ Pure and undefiled religion before God and the Father is this: to visit orphans and have a very high paying job.
- ➢ Man looks at outward appearance, but God looks at the pocketbook.
- ➢ If I made more money at my job, all my problems would go away.
- ➢ I should feel superior to anyone who makes less money than me.

The Truth: You don't need a high paying job to have a successful life. A truly successful person: 1) Seeks first God's kingdom – This creates a release of provision on earth (Matthew 6:33); but, more importantly, causes us to store up treasure in heaven (Matthew 6:20). 2) Loves others – 1 Corinthians 13 love is the pinnacle of Christian success. Truly successful people love well and prioritize healthy relationships. 3) Lives "on assignment" from God – We succeed when we do what God has called us to do. This includes believing our influence is not only for now but also for impacting future generations of families and others.

Strategies for Overcoming This Lie:

1. **Know that the quality of our lives results from the quality of our commitments, not how big our salary is** – Commitment to Jesus, family and biblically based core values will cause enduring success.

2. **Embrace the process of advancing in life** – A butterfly needs the struggle of getting out of the cocoon to become strong. In the same way, the challenges of moving forward in life allow us to build the spiritual muscles needed for our great life assignments ahead.

3. **Pursue increase and promotion in life, but do it God's way** – There is nothing wrong with desiring and pursuing a higher paying job, but we need to realize that becoming prosperous in our souls is the key to seeing increase in our circumstances (3 John 1:2).

Declarations to Renew Your Mind: 1) Jesus thinks I am valuable; therefore, I am. 2) I am doing a great work for God. 3) I am advancing in my career, but the Lord also meets my needs from other sources.

Let's Just Laugh at This Lie

My Expectations Have Nothing to Do With My Experience

Laughable Assumptions Behind This Lie:

> ➤ Because I am predestined to have the life I have, what I believe makes no difference at all in my life experience.

> ➤ When my mind is renewed, nothing is transformed.

> ➤ I refuse to proclaim positive expectations because I don't want people to think I am part of the "name it and claim it," "blab it and grab it" crowd.

> ➤ Those who have high expectations will only be disappointed.

> ➤ When Jesus said, "According to your faith, so be it;" it was not a truth for everyone, but just for the one He was speaking to.

> ➤ If I expect to be rejected, it won't affect people's attitudes toward me.

The Truth: Expectation is another word for faith, and our faith makes a difference in what we experience. The book of Mark makes this clear: 1) "When Jesus saw their faith, He said to the paralytic, 'Son, your sins are forgiven you'" (Mark 2:5). 2) "And He said to her, 'Daughter, your faith has made you well. Go in peace, and be healed of your affliction'" (Mark 5:34). 3) "Jesus said to him, 'If you can believe, all things *are* possible to him who believes'" (Mark 9:23). 4) "Then Jesus said to him, 'Go your way; your faith has made you well'" (Mark 10:52). 5) "Therefore I say to you, whatever things you ask when you pray, believe that you receive *them,* and you will have *them*" (Mark 11:24).

Strategies for Overcoming This Lie:

1. **Embrace doctrines of hope** – We serve a "whoever" God. "Whoever calls on the name of the Lord will be saved" (Romans 10:13). Being "saved" is receiving eternal life and includes deliverance, healing, wholeness and abundant blessings. Every person can <u>experience</u> every aspect of salvation. There is no partiality with God (Romans 2:11).

2. **Feed your hope** – Hope is the confident expectation that good is coming. Those who intentionally feed on testimonies, God's promises and New Covenant truth will increase their positive expectancy.

3. **Know that your experience will catch up to your beliefs** – Mark 11:24 tells us to pray, believe and then we will receive. One powerful way to upgrade our believing is to increase our hearing of truth (Romans 10:17). Just as Abraham became fully convinced of the promise (Romans 4:21), so can we. Then we will experience our own promises.

Declarations to Renew Your Mind: 1) My positive expectancy (faith) causes me to experience God's promises. 2) I am an extremely optimistic person. 3) I hear, believe and receive.

Let's Just Laugh at This Lie

If My Ministry Does Not Appear Successful, Then it is Not

Laughable Assumptions Behind This Lie:

> ➤ Without current outward success in ministry, I am a failure in my calling.
> ➤ Those who plant and water are not successful, but those who reap harvests are very successful.
> ➤ Noah was a failure until the flood validated his ark ministry.
> ➤ Only ministries that have a lot of people and money are successful.
> ➤ If my ministry has unresolved issues, it has obviously failed.
> ➤ My obedience to God is unsuccessful unless people celebrate me.
> ➤ In the Bible, God waited for people to approve someone before He did.

The Truth: God's measurement for success is different than the standard used by most people. 1) David was thought to be unsuccessful by his dad, his brothers and King Saul when he was probably the most successful person alive in God's view (1 Samuel 16 and 17). 2) Those who truly love are more successful than those who do great spiritual things but have not love (1 Corinthians 13). 3) We are winning in God's eyes when we identify what part of Christ's body we are, and then function faithfully in that capacity—even if it does not seem spectacular to others (1 Corinthians 12:14-31).

Strategies for Overcoming This Lie:

1. **Be more planting focused than harvest focused** – We overcome the draining effects of unresolved issues by believing we are in God's will and then strategically planting for future harvest. "Let us not grow weary while doing good, for in due season we shall reap if we do not lose heart" (Galatians 6:9).

2. **Overcome comparing yourself to others** – You are not called to do what someone else is doing. Yes, learn all you can and improve in every way possible, but ultimately you must do your ministry in faith and with a sense of destiny. Those who believe they are successful will dramatically increase their likelihood of significant achievements.

3. **Know that great priorities create great ministries** – There is nothing wrong with having an outwardly great ministry, but it cannot become our obsession. True success will come from having great priorities and commitments. Sustained outer victory results from focusing more on the depth of our lives than the breadth of ministry.

Declarations to Renew Your Mind: 1) I am doing a great work for God and am successful in ministry. 2) I play a key part in worldwide kingdom advancement. 3) My priorities and commitments make me an outstanding leader.

Let's Just Laugh at This Lie
Nobody Around Here Wants to Become a Christian

Laughable Assumptions Behind This Lie:
- ➢ God's love is not drawing people to Himself anymore.
- ➢ Prayers for the unsaved are not working at all.
- ➢ The deception in peoples' hearts is too great for God to break through.
- ➢ Everyone that will ever be saved here has already accepted Jesus.
- ➢ God wills that none should perish, except the people in my town. He really doesn't like them.
- ➢ If I don't see people give their lives to Christ, it means that God is not doing anything in the lives of those around me.

The Truth: Even unlikely people are being drawn to salvation right now. Consider these examples: 1) Zealots in other religions – Saul, who became Paul, had a heart being prepared for a dramatic conversion while he was the most anti-Christian on the planet (Acts 9). 2) Governmental officials – The Ethiopian eunuch's heart was hungry for truth, and he was reading scripture before he was saved (Acts 8:26-39). 3) Hardcore occultists – They got dramatically saved in Ephesus after witnessing a display of the power of God (Acts 19:17-20). 4) Whole families – The Philippian jailer came to work like any other day but left with his whole household being saved (Acts 16:23-34). 5) Mass gatherings – The 3,000 Jews thought they were coming to Jerusalem for the Feast of Pentecost, but they were actually being set up for their spiritual conversion (Acts 2).

Strategies for Overcoming This Lie:
1. **Believe that the people in your life are being prepared for a God encounter** – Not only believe that God is drawing them to Himself but also believe as Peter's shadow healed people (Acts 5:15-16), we have divine influence on those who get close to us. We will see more conversions as we strengthen our beliefs about others wanting Jesus.
2. **Partner with and participate in evangelism and discipleship ministries** – Paul told Timothy, "Do the work of an evangelist" (2 Timothy 4:5). Timothy was exhorted to find a way to impact the unsaved with the gospel—even though it was apparently not his strength.
3. **Find the "son of peace"** – There is a key person in every family, group, city or region that will be God's catalyst for other souls to be saved. Jesus told the seventy to look for such a one to focus their ministry toward (Luke 10:5-6). We would be wise to do the same.

Declarations to Renew Your Mind: 1) Many around me are on the verge of getting saved. 2) Powerful conversions are common in my area. 3) I find a "son of peace" in every situation.

Let's Just Laugh at This Lie
I Am Not Educated or Smart Enough

Laughable Assumptions Behind This Lie:

> God never uses uneducated or under-qualified people for great things.

> If I do not have a college degree, I am an inferior person whose opinions should not be taken seriously.

> The Apostle Paul was more interested in speaking to the intellect of people than in giving a demonstration of the Spirit's power.

> Intelligence is more important than wisdom.

> The spirit of wisdom and revelation only comes to well-educated people.

> God cannot use me unless I speak with eloquence.

> God never downloads to people supernatural wisdom and strategies.

The Truth: God qualifies the called even if they don't seem impressive to the world. 1) Amos was not a professional prophet and was never trained to be; yet, he has impacted generations through his writings (Amos 7:14-15; 9:11-15). 2) Peter and John were unschooled, ordinary men, but they astounded the elite of their day (Acts 4:5-13). 3) Noah did not have a "How to Build an Ark" manual or a degree in ark building, but God gave him step-by-step instructions to do so (Genesis 6:14-22). 4) When Jesus chose his disciples, he chose ordinary men to change the world (Mark 1:16-20; 2:14).

Strategies for Overcoming This Lie:

1. **Pursue wisdom and understanding** – It is a powerful step in life to further your education by every means possible. Yes, even though God can make a way regardless of our educational level, the Bible encourages us to get wisdom and understanding (Proverbs 4:5, 7; 16:16).

2. **Become secure in your identity in Christ** – Ultimately, it is not outward factors such as wealth, education, appearance or popularity that determines the quality of our lives; but it is coming to Christ and believing who He says we are. This is more valuable than gold.

3. **Increase your faith to believe for the impossible** – Faith is a greater force than intelligence. Jesus said, "All things are possible to him who believes" (Mark 9:23). The relentless renewing of our minds with truth creates supernatural transformation (Romans 12:2).

Declarations to Renew Your Mind: 1) God has fully qualified me to change the world. 2) I pursue and live by God's wisdom; therefore, doors of favor and opportunity continually open before me. 3) I learn things easily, have a great memory, and am continuously expanding in wisdom and understanding. 4) People are astounded by my wisdom and knowledge.

Let's Just Laugh at This Lie

I Do Not Have the Gift of Healing or Miracles

Laughable Assumptions Behind This Lie:

> ➢ My past experience defines what gifts I have, not the Bible.

> ➢ If a healing or miracle has never been done through me, it means that I do not have the gift of healing or miracles.

> ➢ God, in His sovereignty, has selected only a few people to perform miracles, and I am not one of them.

> ➢ All who operate in healing have healed everyone 100% of the time.

> ➢ Unless I receive an impartation from a well-known revivalist, I cannot operate in healing or miracles.

The Truth: We all have a healing and miracle ministry. 1) Every believer has a supernatural ministry waiting to manifest. "And these signs will follow those who believe . . . they will lay hands on the sick, and they will recover" (Mark 16:17-18). 2) Even the deacons (those assigned to wait on tables) in Acts had a supernatural ministry (Acts 6:1-8; 8:4-8). 3) 1 Corinthians 14:1 tells us to "desire spiritual gifts" (which includes miracles and healing). God would not ask us to desire something unless it is available to us. 4) In John 20:21, Jesus said, "As the Father has sent Me, I also send you." Here is what the Father sent Jesus to do, "God anointed Jesus of Nazareth with the Holy Spirit and with power, who went about doing good and healing all who were oppressed by the devil, for God was with Him" (Acts 10:38). This is our assignment, and there is grace to do it.

Strategies for Overcoming This Lie:

1. **Believe spiritual gifts are for everyone (including you)** – Can you imagine someone saying, "I wish God had given me the gift of salvation; but He did not, so I won't be going to heaven." That would be ridiculous. Yet, many Christians use the same reasoning for spiritual gifts. Just as we receive our salvation by faith, we receive spiritual gifts by faith.

2. **Declare you have all the gifts now, even if they have not manifested yet** – An apple tree does not wait until apples hang on its branches to call itself an apple tree. Its DNA reveals apples are emerging. Our DNA has healing and miracles in it. Let's declare it now.

3. **Start walking in healing and miracles** – Just as a toddler learns to walk, we grow into activating our gifts by being trained, taking risks and not giving up when there seems to be failure.

Declarations to Renew Your Mind: 1) I have the gifts of healing and miracles. 2) God supernaturally uses me to help others. 3) I am a difference maker.

Let's Just Laugh at This Lie
Money is the Root of All Evil

Laughable Assumptions Behind This Lie:

➢ It makes God happy when His children are poor and living in lack.

➢ I should not expect abundant finances to do the Great Commission.

➢ It is always evil for a person to want more money.

➢ The wealth of the wicked is being stored up for the wicked.

➢ God giving Solomon money was actually a trap and a punishment.

➢ God wants us to prosper in every area of life except finances.

➢ Jesus loves the poor, but dislikes those who have become rich.

➢ In the Parable of the Talents (Matthew 25:14-29), God did not really expect them to increase the talents (money) they were given.

➢ I should feel guilty about having a good paycheck.

The Truth: God liberally provides for those who put His kingdom and His righteousness first. 1) Solomon received great wealth after he prioritized spiritual wisdom (1 Kings 3:10-15). 2) Job's entire estate was doubled when he was restored (Job 42:12-17). 3) Abraham was wealthy and considered as one who pleased God. His "blessing" has been released to us (Hebrews 11:8-20; Galatians 3:13-14). 4) 2 Corinthians 9:6-12 implores us to believe for "an abundance for every good work" and reveals spiritual keys to make it happen.

Strategies for Overcoming This Lie:

1. **Realize that it is the *love* of money that is a root of evil** – We see in 1 Timothy 6:10 that the *love* of money is the problem, not money itself. As we learn to possess money without it possessing us, we will position ourselves for financial increase. Radical generosity is a main antidote to the "love of money" and also a means to great provision.

2. **Become convinced that you cannot do the Great Commission (Matthew 28:18-20) without significant finances** – The call to "go into all the world" implies we will have considerable resources. Overcome any double-mindedness about significant financial increase coming.

3. **Seek the Kingdom and His righteousness (Matthew 6:33)** – It is vital to know that to pursue "His righteousness" is to believe that we are 100% righteous and thus worthy to be blessed. We shouldn't focus on a negative (trying to not love money), but instead embrace our true identity in Christ to create healthy and empowering attitudes about money.

Declarations to Renew Your Mind: 1) God wants to financially bless me. 2) I am righteous and worthy to be financially blessed. 3) I have an abundance for every good work to fulfill the Great Commission.

Let's Just Laugh at This Lie
This Area is Spiritually Hard Ground

Laughable Assumptions Behind This Lie:

➤ The ten spies, not Joshua and Caleb, were right in their assessment that the Promised Land was a spiritually difficult place (Numbers 13-14).

➤ The beliefs of Christians about an area have nothing to do with the level of spiritual breakthrough in it.

➤ God really doesn't like this area because of its sinful history.

➤ When people come here, the open heaven over them closes.

➤ Continually hearing and saying, "This area is hard for the gospel" won't affect our beliefs or the future experience of this geographical region.

➤ Ezekiel should have concluded that the valley of dry bones was an impossible location for spiritual breakthrough (Ezekiel 37).

➤ Demonic strongholds over this region will render my ministry ineffective.

➤ True prophets will try to convince people how spiritually difficult certain locations are.

The Truth: Every area Is completely ready for spiritual transformation because Christians carry an "open heaven" that sets people free wherever they go. 1) Joshua was told, "Every place that the sole of your foot will tread upon I have given you" (Joshua 1:3). He was to be confident for kingdom advancement because of God's promises. We are to be even more confident now because the "least" Christian is greater than anyone in the Old Testament (Matthew 11:11). 2) The 120 on the day of Pentecost turned the world upside down in a place that had a religious stronghold (Acts 2). 3) Ephesus was a hedonistic place, steeped in the occult, but Paul's life and ministry transformed it (Acts 19).

Strategies for Overcoming This Lie:

1. **Stop agreeing with the experience of your area** – We don't deny past difficulties, but we cannot define our region by its experience. If we do, we create strongholds in beliefs that will hinder the purposes of God.

2. **Call those things that are not as though they are (Romans 4:17)** – God's "method" of bringing life to a barren place is to call it alive when it still appears to be dead. As we speak life, He brings transformation.

3. **Stay in faith while waiting for complete breakthrough to manifest** – Realize you are part of a vast plan for what God is doing in your area. You are linked to the past and future in bigger ways than you know.

Declarations to Renew Your Mind: 1) God is doing great things in this area. 2) This region is spiritually alive. 3) Greater is He that is in me than he that is in this area.

Let's Just Laugh at This Lie
Women Should Not Expect to be as Powerful as Men
Laughable Assumptions Behind This Lie:

> ➢ As a woman, I cannot expect to be taken seriously.
> ➢ Women were made in God's weak and powerless image.
> ➢ Being a mother is a hindrance to my ministry and me.
> ➢ As a woman, my call in life is to be silent and to serve men.
> ➢ If only I were a male, I could be so much more successful in life.
> ➢ In the kingdom, everyone is free and empowered except women.

The Truth: Powerful women are found all throughout history. Here are some examples in Scripture: 1) Esther's boldness and bravery caused an entire race to be saved (Esther 4:16; 8:5-9). 2) Abigail saved her whole family by her generosity and wisdom (1 Samuel 25:18-35). 3) Naomi's influence of Ruth contributed to Ruth being King David's great-grandmother and a part of the lineage of Jesus (Ruth 3:1-5; 4:18). 4) The woman at the well caused a spiritual breakthrough in Samaria (John 4). 5) Deborah was an incredible leader who brought great victory for God's people (Judges 4, 5). 6) Priscilla and her husband Aquila were great influencers in the early church and are mentioned as a couple seven times in the New Testament—with five of those references having Priscilla listed first.

Strategies for Overcoming This Lie:

1. **Establish a strong biblical foundation to be a powerful woman –** God's original intent was for women to co-reign with men. "God said to them (man and woman), 'Be fruitful and multiply; fill the earth and subdue it; have dominion . . . '" (Genesis 1:27-28). Although there are some seemingly contradictory passages in the New Testament about the role of women, it is clear that women are equal to men in spiritual potential.

2. **Overcome any roots of bitterness –** Strong women are not bitter, but walk in grace and honor. They do not distrust men, nor do they feel they must strive to prove themselves; but they live and minister from a restful confidence that results from knowing who they are in Christ. Powerful women also celebrate the roles of wife and mother.

3. **Intentionally empower women –** A shortcut to experiencing increase in an area is to give away what we desire to have ourselves (Luke 6:37-38). As we empower women, we are empowered in the process.

Declarations to Renew Your Mind: 1) I am a powerful woman who has great impact. 2) I enjoy being just the way God made me. I'm beautiful, healthy, hilarious, active, strong and dynamic. 3) I have healthy relationships with men. 4) I influence many other women to greatness.

Let's Just Laugh at This Lie
I Need To Walk in Fear of the Devil

Laughable Assumptions Behind This Lie:

> ➤ I should expect inescapable spiritual attacks as I move forward in God.
> ➤ If I resist the devil in Jesus' name, he won't flee from me.
> ➤ I should focus more on what the devil is doing than what God has said.
> ➤ "Super Christians" have authority over the devil, but he beats up on people like me whenever he wants.
> ➤ I don't want to make the devil angry, so I should stop pursuing God.
> ➤ Jesus was terrified and frightened of Satan, so I should be, too.
> ➤ I need to worry about God giving Satan permission to ravage my life.

The Truth: We have been given authority over all the power of the enemy. Yes, it is foolish to ignore the devil's reality, but the Bible calls us to not be afraid of him. 1) "He who is in you is greater than he who is in the world" (1 John 4:4). 3) Jesus has given us "authority . . . over all the power of the enemy, and nothing shall by any means hurt [us]" (Luke 10:19). 4) Like the psalmist, we are protected from the enemy by abiding "under the shadow of the Almighty" (Psalm 91). 5) When we resist the devil, he has to flee from us (James 4:7). 6) We become an "undevourable" Christian by resisting the devil through being "steadfast in the faith" (1 Peter 5:8-9). 7) Paul told the Romans that God would crush Satan under their feet (Romans 16:20), and He will do the same for us.

Strategies for Overcoming This Lie:

1. **Believe that Jesus' death and resurrection have disarmed the power of the devil (Colossians 2:15)** – Jesus took the keys of authority back from him and gave them to His church (Matthew 16:17-19).

2. **Place more faith in God's ability to protect than the devil's ability to harm or deceive** – Determine to talk more about God's protection than about Satan's attacks. We will see more of what we regularly speak about because faith (both positive and negative) comes by hearing (Romans 10:17).

3. **Meditate on scriptures concerning God's goodness and protection over your life** – "As [a man] thinks in his heart, so is he" (Proverbs 23:7). A right focus in thoughts helps draw God's promises to us.

Declarations to Renew Your Mind: 1) Greater is He that is in me than he that is in the world. 2) No weapon formed against me will prosper. 3) I am covered in God's protection. 4) The enemy has been defeated by what Jesus did on the cross. 5) The devil was stripped of any legal right to harm me.

Let's Just Laugh at This Lie
I Am Too Busy to do Things Right

Laughable Assumptions Behind This Lie:

➤ Because I am a victim to my busy schedule, I cannot expect to be loving, respectful or to follow through on what I say I will do.

➤ It is more important to get things done than to do things right.

➤ If I am doing something important, then the end justifies the means.

➤ Jesus was "busy" about His father's business, and that is why He made so many mistakes in His ministry.

➤ Jesus was wrong when He said that faithfulness to small responsibilities is what is needed for bigger things to be entrusted to us.

➤ Having good priorities is not nearly as important as staying very busy.

The Truth: Powerful priorities, not excessive busyness, bring long-term benefits. 1) Haggai reveals the benefits of doing that which is most important, and the folly of becoming busy with the less crucial issues of life (Haggai 1:3-11). 2) The book of Proverbs is a gold mine of nuggets to inspire us to put integrity, godly speech and purity above the pursuit of success. 3) The institution of the Sabbath reveals that doing more is not the answer. We are not to legalistically observe it, but the Sabbath principle is a profound spiritual law to comprehend as we seek increase in our lives.

Strategies for Overcoming This Lie:

1. **Overcome the tyranny of the urgent** – It is unlikely that anyone will say on their deathbed, "I wish I would have spent more time at the office and less time with my family." The imperatives of life (God, family, integrity, etc.) don't scream for attention until there is some sort of crisis—while less important matters appear more urgent than they really are.

2. **Develop non-negotiable convictions** – Daniel kept praying to God even when it was against the law because it "was his custom since early days" (Daniel 6:10). We too are to firmly prioritize time for God, family, rest and the distinctive calling on our lives. It is easier to say no to lesser choices if we have already said yes to higher things.

3. **Work hard from a place of deep spiritual rest** – "He who has entered His rest has himself also ceased from his works as God *did* from His" (Hebrews 4:10). We walk in God's rest by trusting in the finished work of the cross, having a healthy identity and believing we impact the unseen realm in significant and positive ways.

Declarations to Renew Your Mind: 1) I walk in Hebrews 4 spiritual rest. 2) I do great things in God with a lifestyle that is full of integrity and love. 3) I am committed to that which is really important.

Let's Just Laugh at This Lie
It May Work Somewhere Else, But It Won't Work Here

Laughable Assumptions Behind This Lie:

> ➤ There is something uniquely wrong with this area.
> ➤ My city is under a spiritually closed heaven because of its unworthiness.
> ➤ God is too busy to visit my city.
> ➤ It only works in places where I am not present.
> ➤ My city is not a hotspot for revival and never could be.
> ➤ God is not doing anything to set up my city for transformation.
> ➤ God is picky as to where He shows up and does extraordinary things.

The Truth: God is no respecter of person or area. Scriptural examples are bountiful: 1) Nineveh was in a state of moral decay and wickedness, but it quickly turned from sin to God (Jonah 1-3). 2) A prison had a sudden revival when Paul and Silas worshipped, and everyone bound was supernaturally set free (Acts 16). 3) Paul performed unusual miracles in Ephesus, a city widely known for its idolatry. The people burned their magic books (worth about 50,000 days of wages) and demons fled (Acts 19). 4) The people dwelling in Decapolis begged Jesus to leave after the man with the Legion was restored, but because of that man's testimony, a crowd welcomed Jesus when He returned (Mark 5, 7). 5) In a place as unlikely as a stable, God Himself took on flesh to restore relationship with His sons and daughters (Luke 2).

Strategies for Overcoming This Lie:

1. **Understand personal transformation creates city transformation –** Whatever His good pleasure is for your area, it's God at work in you that gives you the power to see it accomplished (Philippians 2:13). Once we encounter Him, we become an encounter for others (Mark 16:17-18). We "leak" the very knowledge of God to those around us (2 Corinthians 2:14).

2. **Use your spiritual authority –** We don't have to beg God to do something that He's already given us authority to do. He made us His home and told us to heal the sick, cast out devils, cleanse the lepers, and do even greater things than Jesus did (Matthew 10:8, John 14:12). We are region igniters.

3. **Pursue excellent stewardship –** The spiritual keys to cities are gained through faithful stewardship of the opportunities that God has given us now (Luke 19:11-27). Revival is attracted to the areas where God's people are doing small things in a great way.

Declarations to Renew Your Mind: 1) It is impossible for this city to remain the same because God, at work in me, is being released through me. 2) I am consistently leaking the life-giving knowledge of God. 3) The presence of God richly and thickly covers my city/workplace/home.

Let's Just Laugh at This Lie
I Will Never Get Out of Debt

Laughable Assumptions Behind This Lie:
- ➢ Jesus took my debt of sin on the cross, but I will have to get out of financial debt by myself.
- ➢ Because I caused this debt, God is frustrated and won't help me.
- ➢ There are no solutions for this level of debt.
- ➢ I missed a tithe ten years ago; therefore I am cursed with debt.
- ➢ There is no hope for my finances because of who is in my family.
- ➢ Saving money is sinful, so I should quickly spend whatever I receive.
- ➢ I should not get my hopes up that I could get out of debt.
- ➢ My poor financial decisions have been pressed down, good measure and are running over into everlasting debt.

The Truth: God has already made provision for us to be saved from financial debt. 1) Jesus took our financial debt on the cross. "He (Jesus) was rich, yet for your sakes He became poor, that you through His poverty might become rich" (2 Corinthians 8:9). 2) God's heart is to meet all our needs, including debt cancellation. "And my God shall supply all your need according to His riches in glory by Christ Jesus" (Philippians 4:19). 3) God has a specific wisdom for each of us to get out of debt. "If any of you lacks wisdom, let him ask of God, who gives to all liberally and without reproach, and it will be given to him" (James 1:5).

Strategies for Overcoming This Lie:
1. **Believe your debt has been paid in full** – Just as none of us are worthy (apart from Christ) to have our sins cancelled, no one deserves to have their debt cancelled either, but Jesus took our debt on the cross so we can walk in blessing and influence. We are to use our spiritual authority to confidently rebuke debt and receive abundant provision.
2. **Break off the debt mentality** – Chronic financial debt is often a symptom of a "debt mentality" that impulsively sacrifices the future for current needs or wants (e.g. spiritual debt, time debt, relationship debt, emotional debt, health debt, etc.). As we partner with God, He will cause us to invest in our future, not take from it.
3. **Receive God's specific strategy for you** – There is supernatural wisdom available. We don't need more money as much as we need a strategy from heaven. Activate the James 1:5 principle now.

Declarations to Renew Your Mind: 1) I am debt free. 2) I increasingly buy items with cash. 3) The debt mentality is broken off of me. 4) I invest extravagantly into the future. 5) I free others from financial debt.

Let's Just Laugh at This Lie
It Is Too Late for My Nation

Laughable Assumptions Behind This Lie:

> ➤ There are no solutions—even God doesn't know what to do.
> ➤ Past and current prayers for our nation are not working.
> ➤ It is impossible for a transforming spiritual revival to occur here.
> ➤ A nation cannot be saved in a day.
> ➤ There are few (if any) people that God has placed in strategic places.
> ➤ The gates of hell have prevailed against the church in my nation.
> ➤ One revived and anointed person cannot change a nation.

The Truth: Nations can turn around quickly. 1) The immoral people of Nineveh surprisingly responded to Jonah's message and things turned around (see book of Jonah). 2) 2 Chronicles 7:14 reveals the powerful influence believers can have to see their nation healed. 3) The ungodly king Nebuchadnezzar had a nation-impacting encounter with God through the influence of Daniel and three other young men (Daniel 3:26-30; 4:34-37). 4) The fortunes of the nation of Israel changed in a day when David killed Goliath (1 Samuel 17). 5) The story of the dry bones in Ezekiel reveals that "very dry" and dead-looking nations can come alive. 6) A study of revivals in the last 2,000 years will build faith that spiritual transformation can occur in backslidden nations.

Strategies for Overcoming This Lie:

1. **Stir up hope for your nation** – In Ezekiel 37, God asked, "Can these bones live?" The answer was obviously yes, even though it looked impossible. The important question is not how bad a nation is (how dry the bones are), but whether someone has hope that the nation can live. Nothing is impossible with God.

2. **Implement 2 Chronicles 7:14 in your life** – Grow in each aspect of this verse (humility, prayer, seeking God's face and repentance). Find people to partner with in these things to see your nation healed.

3. **Support ministries and people that are making a difference in your nation** – Become a strength to those who are bringing change (and those who will bring transformation in the future). Identify your role, and be faithful.

Declarations to Renew Your Mind: 1) God is moving powerfully in my nation. 2) The church is revived in my country. 3) God has powerful people in every aspect of society that are bringing transformation.

Let's Just Laugh at This Lie
One Person Cannot Change the World

Laughable Assumptions Behind This Lie:

➢ God has predestined a few, select people with the ability to change the world, and I am not one of them.

➢ Jesus changed the world, but He wasn't serious when He said that we would do greater things than Him.

➢ David, Moses, Abraham, Esther and Peter changed the world because they did not have any weaknesses or negative circumstances to face.

➢ It is too late for anyone to change the world, so we should not try.

➢ Biblical stories of people changing the world are just for our enjoyment—not as a testimony to inspire us to do the same.

➢ God wants things to fall apart in the end times, so He gets irritated if we try to change the world.

The Truth: Every person should believe they have the potential to change the world. Those in the Bible were not predestined to do what they did. They had a nature like us (James 5:17). 1) Paul responded to God, and his Spirit-infused intelligence and zeal changed the course of history. 2) Esther used her favor to save the Jewish people. 3) Abraham left the familiar, and his beliefs altered history. 4) Moses responded to an inner compulsion to be different and thus saved his people. 5) Noah prepared for the future and saved the world from extinction. 6) Mary became impregnated with God's solution for mankind. 7) David's courage, faithfulness and passion for God still influences us today.

Strategies for Overcoming This Lie:

1. **Know the incredible power of faith** – "All things *are* possible to him who believes" (Mark 9:23). "For with God nothing will be impossible" (Luke 1:37). "He who believes in Me, the works that I do he will do also; and greater *works* than these he will do" (John 14:12).

2. **Feed on the stories of people who have made a difference** – Study about influential Bible characters. Learn about others in history that did great exploits. This will stir up faith and endurance to make a difference.

3. **Despise not the day of small beginnings** – Big accomplishments result from a series of small steps. Realize, too, that promises and influence are not just for our lifetime but live on through our descendents.

Declarations to Renew Your Mind: 1) I am positively changing the world, and my influence is increasing. 2) I will do greater things than Jesus did. 3) I am a person with incredible beliefs. 4) The completion of my world-changing purpose will be accomplished through my descendents.

Other Books by Steve Backlund

<u>**Igniting Faith in 40 Days**</u> – Written with Wendy, this book is ideal for a 40-day negativity fast and to pour "spiritual gasoline" on your faith and hope. It also will help the reader understand the power of declaring truth.

<u>**Cracks in the Foundation**</u> – This writing examines the negative effects of religious tradition that neutralizes the power of God's promises. Its teachings will repair cracks in your faith foundation so that God can build something great through you.

<u>**Possessing Joy**</u> – The joy of the Lord is our strength, and a merry heart is like good medicine. God has called us to serve Him with gladness. This book will give you incredible keys to do so.

<u>**You're Crazy If You DON'T Talk to Yourself**</u> – 'Life is in the power of the tongue" (Proverbs 18:21). Jesus did not just think His way out of the wilderness and neither can you. Like Jesus, we must speak truth to invisible forces and to the mindsets that seek to restrict and defeat us.

<u>**Victorious Mindsets**</u> – What we believe is ultimately more important than what we do. The course of our lives is set by our deepest core beliefs (mindsets). These mindsets are either a stronghold for God's purposes or a playhouse for the enemy of our souls. This book reveals 50 biblical attitudes that are foundational for walking in freedom and power.

<u>**Divine Strategies for Increase**</u> – "But his delight is in the law of the Lord . . . and whatever he does shall prosper" (Psalm 1:3). The Psalmist talks of one whose prime delight is in the law of the Lord. These laws are not to be seen as rules but are spiritual principles to unlock heaven's resources to flow to us and through us. This book reveals the reality of the spirit realm and gives a strategy to increase our talents so we can change the world.

Helpful resources and audio messages by Steve and Wendy Backlund are available at www.ignitedhope.com and www.ibethel.org/store (go to "browse by author" – Steve Backlund). You can find out where the Backlunds are speaking by going to the ignitedhope website.

Made in the USA
San Bernardino, CA
01 August 2015